Engendering Church

Engendering Church

Women, Power,
and the AME Church

Jualynne E. Dodson

ROWMAN & LITTLEFIELD PUBLISHERS, INC.
Lanham • Boulder • New York • Oxford

ROWMAN & LITTLEFIELD PUBLISHERS, INC.

Published in the United States of America
by Rowman & Littlefield Publishers, Inc.
4720 Boston Way, Lanham, Maryland 20706
www.rowmanlittlefield.com

12 Hid's Copse Road
Cumnor Hill, Oxford OX2 9JJ, England

British Library Cataloguing in Publication Information Available

Library of Congress Cataloging-in-Publication Data

Dodson, Jualynne E.
    Engendering church : women, power, and the AME Church / Jualynne E. Dodson.
    p. cm.
    Includes bibliographical references and index.
    ISBN 0-8476-9380-5 (alk. paper)—ISBN 0-8476-9381-3 (pbk : alk. paper)
    1. African Methodist Episcopal Church—History. 2. Women in church work—African
Methodist Episcopal Church. 3. African American women—Religious life—History. 4.
Methodist women—United States—History. 5. African American Methodists—History. I.
Title.

BX8443 .D63 2002
287'.83–dc21   2001031793

Printed in the United States of America

⊗™ The paper used in this publication meets the minimum requirements of
American National Standard for Information Sciences—Permanence of Paper
for Printed Library Materials, ANSI/NISO Z39.48–1992.

This book is dedicated to those who have gone before and made me possible: Angella, Floria, and Bessie. To those who carry forth with big footsteps: Lazy Bones, "Mis" Harris, Lou Birda, Flora, Sheryll, Alyce, and my mother, Flora. It is also for those who wish to "crawl back through history" to understand what really happened. Thank you one and all!

—Jualynne Elizabeth White Dodson

Contents

Introduction

Past Is Prologue

Before we unlock the future
we must first find keys to the past.

In August 2000, the African Methodist Episcopal Church, the largest centrally organized denomination of African Americans in the United States, if not the world, convened the forty-sixth quadrennial General Conference, the legislative body of the Church. At that gathering, two women stood to be elected as the first of their gender to the office of bishop of the denomination. The election of a woman bishop may stand as a first for independent African American denominations. However, the very possibility of prominent service by women in the AME Church required more than a century of struggle to accomplish.

In 1900, Mrs. Sara Hatcher Duncan was appointed president of the Women's Home and Foreign Missionary Society of the AME Church. She had been general superintendent of the society since 1897 and would be its president for the next ten years. Mrs. Duncan would use her leadership position to agitate against the clergy's lack of support for local activities of the gendered missionary societies. Although firmly entrenched in Euro-American ideas of "civilized" behavior, Sara Duncan would become an outspoken critic of the male leadership and demonstrably "feminist" in her stance. She publicly acknowledged the explosive and divisive North-South tensions that plagued the denomination's leaders

1

as well as members. She invited the entire denomination to watch her southern missionary society outstrip its northern counterpart in size and in the quality of its work. Further, she proclaimed the right of women to full participation in the Church. Sara Duncan expressed these ideas publicly and to the highest levels of the denomination's governing hierarchy.

African Methodist women had earned an outspoken advocate like Sara Hatcher Duncan. Her challenges to the Church's decision-making assemblies represented women's increased use of the power they had acquired throughout the nineteenth century, particularly through the mechanisms of their gender-specific organizations. Their goal, which was now stated more openly than in the preceding century, was nothing short of structural change in church governance. As president of the Women's Home and Foreign Missionary Society, Sara Duncan personified the independence of black churchwomen; she also represented what women's power in the AME Church had already achieved.

Notwithstanding, women did not use the power and authority of organizational position to bring about changes for women in the AME Church. Their power rested in their ability to negotiate in a dynamic, reciprocal, and intricate social process. They had done so for eighty-four years in the preceding century; slowly but surely they had introduced women and their interests into three Church positions and two missionary societies. The provocative ten-year presidency of Mrs. Duncan culminated a century of organizational accomplishments on behalf of women and exemplified the results of women's involvement in the complex power relations of an African American denomination. The nineteenth century was a prologue to twentieth-century accomplishments, as the twentieth century was to be a prologue to women's twenty-first-century accession to the episcopacy.

When the AME Church was founded in 1816, it had no official place for women. Men held all offices in the three labyrinthine and overlapping structural units—the ministry, the laity, and the conferences. The structure would not change with regard to women for the first fifty-two years of Church life. No one questioned the gender exclusivity at the time, 1816 to 1868, but in the latter third of the century determination and behind-the-scenes work established the positions of stewardess, female evangelist, and deaconess, and founded two women's missionary societies. The changes did not happen because churchmen were cooperative and eager to include women in hierarchy; it took hard, sustained effort by women like Mary A. Prout, Jarena Lee, Zilpha Elaw, Pricilla Baltimore, Amanda Berry Smith, and Sara Duncan. There were many battles and many losses before 1900, and it was not until the turn of the twenty-first century that Vashti McKenzie would be elected a bishop of the AME Church.

As an African American woman scholar, I have a personal interest in the power, processes, and circumstances that brought about the new gendered arrangements in the AME Church. Through this book I explore the interplay of social processes like the acquisition of power and pose several sociological questions regarding the historical realities of nineteenth-century AME women. For example, in what categories of social activity did black women acquire power in their Church? By what processes did they acquire these prerequisites, and how did they exercise their power within the all-male hierarchy? What were the social, cultural, and structural realignments that produced a Sara Hatcher Duncan, who assumed the right and authority to confront that hierarchy with the sexist misconduct of its male clergy? These questions are significant, because over the nineteenth century AME women, working behind the scenes, slowly and steadily brought the denomination to include positions for women—as evidenced by Sara Duncan. Unfortunately, unless women hold such positions, they are overlooked. Even when they achieve structural status, organizational change is regularly attributed to others, not to women's exercise of power. It is my intention to reveal women as powerful actors and implementers of changes in denominational structures.

Sociologist Patricia Hill Collins has made an important contribution to our ability to conceptualize the distinctive character of African American women's participation in U.S. organizations. Her concept of the "double-bind, double-jeopardy" nature of race and gender for African American women is helpful for thinking about churchwomen's struggles against racism as well as against sexism. Most students of the Black Church see it as a bastion of male privilege and gender discrimination, but this is not the whole story. Traditionally, the Black Church, throughout its variety of denominations and congregations, has been a social space where women functioned in key leadership roles—both moral and operational leadership.

Equally significant, African American women have fought notable battles to establish their particular church bodies as viable social institutions that could help to improve the living conditions of blacks in the United States. These struggles are especially remarkable because women were simultaneously fighting against the racism of white privilege in U.S. society as well as struggling to guarantee the inclusion of women in the very church structures and institutional arrangements they were building. Each of these was a battlefront of social confrontation, and black women waged all three parts of the struggle simultaneously. Too often the multisided confrontations of churchwomen lessen our ability to appreciate and analyze the contest against sexist exclusion within the Black Church. In this book, I want to tell the whole story of the many AME women who, like Sara Duncan, altered their denomination's organizational structure to include women. It is the story of women, power, and the AME Church, of African American churchwomen accumulating the sources of power—membership, organization, and resources—to create a gender-inclusive body. These sources of power gave AME women an ability to seize opportunities and to implement their purposes even when there was opposition.

This story of women, power, and the AME Church includes their collaborative work with an all-male hierarchy, as well as their more radical activities that challenged and changed Church structure. There were women who put forth extraordinary individual efforts; women who merged their energies with those of other women; women who were indispensable to Church growth but are yet unknown; women who assertively and consciously worked to be included in the Church, and other women, with more spiritual agendas, for whom structural inclusion was insignificant. But when the entire story of the nineteenth century is told, women are seen to have compelled the denomination to create structural positions for their gender.

Engendering Church is a book about power as much as the creation by women of a denomination. I begin with their presence at the birth of the very idea of an independent African American denomination, and with their participation in the early formation of a religious association. Women were definitely present during these originating events in the late eighteenth century, but histories of the AME Church rarely discuss them or their contributions. Chapter 1, therefore, presents the role of women in the earliest origins of an African Methodist congregation and of the AME denomination. They actively protested discrimination in Church worship, supported legal petitions for congregational autonomy, gathered individuals to form local churches, united congregations into a denomination, and did all that was necessary to bring a noble idea of independence and self-determination into embryonic reality. This chapter establishes the magnitude of women's numerical presence in these beginning years, their first actions toward creating a gender-specific organization, and their earliest access to resources.

Chapters 2, 3, and 4 recount women's accumulation of the three sources of power—membership, organization, and resources—and their subsequent challenges to the male hierarchy. I describe details of women's presence and activity in these categories during the denomination's geographic expansion across North America and into international arenas. Despite the many details and specifics that have not previously been included in denominational histories, this is not an exhaustive survey. Rather, I have tried to present a focused image of the times and activities in which AME women were involved.

Chapter 5 focuses on how AME women combined their sources of power to accomplish their goals, but I also remind readers that the works of Evelyn Brooks Higginbotham and Cheryl Townsend Gilkes demonstrate that African American women have altered other denominations as well. Because women in denominations of their studies and this one represent more than half of all black churchwomen in the United States, AME experiences can be considered normative; further, the nineteenth-century experiences of African Methodist women can clarify how black women have used their power without destroying the Black Church as a pivotal institution in the larger African American community. The chapter is concerned with how women used the knowledge they possessed; how they capitalized upon the sources of power to involve themselves in denominational decision making; how they engaged in social processes that reflected the interplay of power in the AME Church while keeping the organization healthy and strong.

Chapter 6 focuses on the gendered space women constructed in the Church by virtue of their membership numbers, network of organizations, and their material and nonmaterial resources. The male leadership officially authorized these spaces when they found that they could not effectively manage women's activities without them. However, through their energies and activities women constructed the gendered spaces on behalf of women.

I return in chapter 7 to Sara Hatcher Duncan, exemplar of churchwomen's nineteenth-century struggles for inclusion, and harbinger of the twentieth- and twenty-first-century gendered African Methodist Episcopal Church. In general, *Engendering Church* recounts women's evolutionary acquisition of power to change the denomination; specifically, however, it identifies and describes the cultural particulars of black churchwomen's feminist activity in the context of American racism, male sexism, and the distinctive African American cultural reality.

1

✦

Formation of a
Religious Organization

PROTEST AND ORGANIZE

As early as 1758, independent-minded African descendants in
North America's mid-Atlantic region chose separate religious
worship rather than tolerate the racial discrimination that accompanied the services of whites.[1] In Philadelphia in 1787, a small
group of women and men reached the end of their tolerance of the
white Christians of St. George Methodist Episcopal Church, and
a historic protest ensued. Among the rebelling African Americans
were Jane Ann Murray, Sarah Dougherty, and Mother Duncan—
we know only her last name—along with Absalom Jones and
Richard Allen, two leaders of the Philadelphia black community.
The white clergy had treated its black members as second-class individuals, as nonbelievers; African American patience reached its
limit one Sunday morning in November. During the successful
struggle for national sovereignty, these Philadelphians had seen
and heard proclamations of liberty and freedom for all and they
too had cultivated a sense of capability for independence. On the
fateful morning, several members knelt in prayer at the front of St.
George's sanctuary. Others were seated in the balcony, seats designated for African Americans. Customarily, there were specified
times for blacks to pray at the front of the church, but for some
unknown reason the parishioners of darker hue were at the altar

7

in prayer this November morning at what a white Church official felt was the wrong time.

The trustee interrupted the kneeling Christians and informed them that they were in the wrong place. Rather than acquiesce to the intrusion on their sacred conversation and retreat to the balcony, those at the altar continued their solemn prayer. The trustee then attempted to physically remove one of the worshippers. The sisters and brothers were talking to God; nobody should disrupt such holy activity, not even to preserve a supposed white superiority. Something had to be done, but what?

Every black person in St. George, including those in the balcony, spontaneously stood up and left the Church. It must have been a dramatic scene as the entire body of African Americans walked out, en masse. No amount of persuasion would make them return. The protesters formed a mutual-aid association for themselves and other black citizens of Philadelphia—the Free African Society.[2]

Historians have tended to emphasize the social-protest aspect of the event, no doubt because of the drama it entailed. However, African Americans also had a spiritual disagreement with the general worship practices of St. George's and of most European American congregations. These were free blacks, not enslaved. Many had practiced Christianity for years, during which they had subordinated their worship preferences to those of white Christians. Now they were ready for worship services that respected them as equal to all other children of God and reflected their spiritual preferences. They had inherited distinct, African American Christian sensibilities, and they wanted a mode of worship that was true to that heritage.

The enslaved ancestors of the protestors were eighteenth-century free American Africans who began a quest for spiritual expression even as they endured the horrifying Middle Passage. The reality of enslavement was all-encompassing, a distinct historical experience that differed from any undergone by whites who also lived in North America. During the seventeenth and early eighteenth centuries, these enslaved Africans and their descendants searched for spiritual release of their emotions, even within the constraints of their bondage. The displaced sons and daughters used fragments of sacred beliefs and practices remembered from their African homelands to begin the quest for expression of their humanity.[3]

In northern and southern colonies, these enslaved people gathered away from the eyes of whites, in secret places of worship in the bush and forests, places called "hush arbors" and "praise houses."[4] As they called and responded to each other in song, dance, and tears, they consecrated the sites and joined themselves with the spiritual unity of all creation. They sang, danced, prayed, appealed, and invoked divine power, calling upon the Creator. Their bodies rocked, heads swayed, feet stamped, and voices moaned—but none too loudly, so as not to arouse the slave masters' attention. These hush arbor practices arose as expressions of their true African identity, not the identity imposed in a white context of European American worship. From these indigenous practices came worship traditions fully embedded in the African-ness of their ancestry and the historicity of their enslavement—traditions specific to American Africans in the United States. The traditions were handed down to the enslaved born in the United States, and they were inherited by the African Americans who would break away from St. George's Church in Philadelphia.

As the eighteenth-century "Great Awakening"[5] gained strength in what would become the United States, many barriers and prohibitions against teaching Christianity to American Africans were loosened. Now the hush-arbor customs encountered Christianity, as even those enslaved in the South were systematically exposed to the faith. The response from the black population was positive; many adopted and practiced the socially accepted religious tradition. An increase in the number of African American traveling deacons and preachers, who articulated the gospel from the perspective of the enslaved, brought an even more rapid increase in the number of free and enslaved converts.[6] However, these new black Christians did not discard their African-derived sensibilities about spirituality and expressive worship when they embraced and adapted Christianity. Eighteenth-century descendants of the Atlantic coast region, free and enslaved, inherited this collective consciousness of an African American Christianity.

Black Christians of 1787 may have attended the worship services of whites, often with whites, but their spiritual needs were not always satisfied. In Philadelphia, Baltimore, Wilmington (Del.), New York, and elsewhere, they desired culturally expressive worship as well as independent governance. Whites did not

sing the mournful dirge chants that African people found mean-
ingful. White worshippers did not make rhythmic body move-
ments, did not respond aloud to sermons, and did not embody
nor allow for the expressive spirit, however Christian, of African
Americans. Independent black churches would not only eliminate
racism from worship but would offer services in a manner that
could satisfy their members' cultural aesthetic. Freedom to worship in their own way was a principle driving the women and
men who protested at Philadelphia's St. George's Church.

Jane Ann Murray and Sarah Dougherty stood up in the balcony
of St. George's Church on that famous Sunday morning in November 1787; they too defiantly walked out of the sanctuary.
They became charter members of the Free African Society. Mrs.
Dougherty was a widow and appears to have been well known in
the black community. She opened her home to the newly formed
society; her home was the regular meeting place for the group
through December 1788.[7] Mrs. Dougherty's home had undoubtedly been inherited from her deceased husband. Neither she nor
the other black women of Philadelphia were rich or financially
well endowed; few African Americans of the period were. Most
were enslaved or had been freed from bondage only a generation
before.

Women of the African Methodist movement could earn a meager income by washing, ironing, sewing, cooking, house cleaning,
or other domestic chores. A few had small retail businesses, and
some were otherwise employed outside of their homes.[8] In the
context of African American economic impoverishment, however,
even the meager income of this minority of free black women,
coupled with the modest inheritances of the widows, could easily
have earned them the social status of "well to do." Setting examples for African Methodists, the women were quick to share their
modest resources for the benefit of the larger black community.

The Free African Society was a mutual-aid association with a
participatory decision-making process. Voting was the mechanism
for making decisions. Moral character and group allegiance were
the only membership criteria, and all members in good standing
were equally eligible to vote on issues that affected the group.
Women's votes helped determine the amount of dues each person
should pay and how the money was to be used. Women voted too

on violations of the society's rules of social conduct. Voting was also the means of determining how food, clothing, and other material goods would be distributed. It was used for decisions about aid to the African American population of Philadelphia. Women were equal participants in these vote-driven decisions on how to exercise the power and authority of the society.[9]

The Free African Society operated successfully following the exodus from St. George, but these pioneers had not separated merely to become a mutual-aid association. They were striving to create a community of African American Christians—a community wherein their understandings about worship could be expressed without social condescension and racial discrimination. They wanted an organized, ritually defined religious practice. Soon society members held a series of discussions about religious tenets and denominational policy. They felt no inherent contradiction between their desire for an independent church and attachment to a white denominational structure. Indeed, in the United States social respectability was associated with white organizational patterns and African Americans living in the United States sought respectability.

Most members of the Free African Society preferred the administrative arrangements of the Protestant Episcopal Church of European Americans. These members formed an independent congregation but chose to remain affiliated with the Episcopalian denomination. A minority, however, felt that the teachings and polity of Wesleyan Methodism, which allowed for more participatory worship and emphasized a systematic program of Christian behavior, were more adaptable to the sentiments and needs of their cultural sisters and brothers. These members, with women clearly represented among them, organized according to the Wesleyan tradition, forming the customary "Methodist class." The African Methodists eventually purchased and refurbished a small Philadelphia blacksmith shop, which they named Bethel African Methodist Church.[10]

In cities other than Philadelphia at the beginning of the nineteenth century, women were also involved in the establishment of independent African Methodist churches. Free blacks in Baltimore, Maryland, became unhappy with the racially separated galleries at Lovely Lane Church. Neither did these independence-minded Christians like having to wait until white communicants had finished before they received the sacrament of Communion. By the time of the renowned 1787 Philadelphia walkout, African Americans in Baltimore were forming a separate Methodist organization and purchasing their own building as well. Annie Dickerson and Mary A. Prout were representative of the group who separated from Lovely Lane and became charter members of the new, independent congregation.[11] Together with charter women of Bethel Philadelphia, they established a pattern wherein women were original participants in denominational affairs, a trend that continued throughout the nineteenth century. We know names of only a few of these trendsetters: Annie Dickerson and Mary A. Prout in Baltimore, and Jane Ann Murray and Mother Duncan of Philadelphia. However, hundreds if not thousands of women were among the original organizers of AME congregations; as charter members they were the pillars upon whom formed local infrastructures, which in turn constructed the denomination.[12]

African Americans adopted the structure of Wesleyan Methodism for their denomination. The arrangement had been brought to the United States from England by Bishop Francis Ashbury, one known to receive African Americans into the community of adherents. Methodism required that members of local congregations be subdivided into smaller, more intimate study groups. These "Methodist classes" ensured that individuals who converted to the tradition learned the practices needed for integration into denominational life. It was normal for women in England and North America to be members of such classes, and they regularly helped in the socialization of new members.

Methodism had other small-group activities that nurtured collective identity and community solidarity—a practice that enhanced the popularity of the tradition in America. For example, Methodist "bands" specialized in singing, praying, and other pastimes related to collective Methodist life. Bands, which were distinctive to Wesleyan Methodism, also sponsored such social activities as picnics, cake sales, pageants, etc. By the middle of the nineteenth century, it was common to find singing bands from several congregations within a region gathering to share, demonstrate, and compare skills. These competitive events reinforced the sense of belonging and membership identity among local congregants, as they enhanced the Methodist reputation as a tradition that built community. Fostering community was a major goal of African Americans, particularly women. Women of the AME Church gladly embraced this community-building aspect of Methodist tradition and then used it to bolster their own struggle for gender equity in the denomination.

"Prayer bands" were another characteristic feature of Methodism. These bands gathered for weekly prayer meetings in which members offered public testimonies of faith, revelation, or Christian conversion. The combination of praying and singing bands, as well as denominational study classes, constituted a closely woven network of face-to-face relationships that integrated new members into local Church life while unifying the surrounding community. These intimate social groupings were instrumental in providing cohesion to African American social life, while simultaneously attracting new Church members. It is no wonder that the women and men of the Philadelphia Free African Society were drawn to Wesleyan Methodism.

During the formative years of the new denomination, African Methodist women were prominent activists in the grassroots work of local congregations. Neighborhood and community-based coordination was the foundation upon which they built a strong reputation in and for the AME Church. Their work, and the women themselves, created African Methodism and became revered legends of Church and community. Stories were told about Mrs. Prout of Baltimore, who was a member when the first congregation "consisted of but nine souls." In later handbills that celebrated origins of the Baltimore church, Annie Dickerson was called an invaluable resource who held the first members steady in their vision of independence and self-determination.[13] Her coaxing, inspiration, and guidance sustained the fledgling pioneers in their departure from the white congregation. Mother Duncan and Wealthy Dorsey of Bethel Church Philadelphia were similarly lauded as organizing a praying band whose reputation was known in and outside the city. Stories would also arise about Hattie Thomas and Mother Shepherd of Philadelphia, who regularly convened Sunday morning prayer meetings in the formative years of African Methodism.[14]

Women, then, were the history and heritage of the denomination. Their reputations accrued the traditional authority that accompanies association with significant historical events. Their traditional authority would be an important asset as African Methodism formed independent congregations and organized into a denomination. Eventually, the formal structure would produce a patriarchal church wherein women had no official positions. However, the hierarchy could not completely disempower women, if only because their traditional, not organizational, authority was well established in the historical consciousness of African Methodism and the larger African American community. This reputation would help prevent the male leadership from taking definitive steps to completely close Church structure to women. The women would acquire other sources of power and take actions that would lead to structural changes to include women.[15]

Few at the close of the eighteenth century gave much attention to the magnitude of organizing an independent black denomination or to ensuring that women were fully involved in the historic work. Nonetheless, impoverished and disenfranchised, these colonial African American women and men dared to step out of white religious worship centers, dared further to organize independent congregations according to their own cultural aesthetic, and even dared to secure legal authorization within the newly formed United States of America.

LEGAL INDEPENDENCE

In 1816, representatives from independent congregations of African Methodism in the middle Atlantic states went to Philadelphia to consolidate their churches into a denomination. The delegates came from Philadelphia, Baltimore, New York, Wilmington (Delaware), and Attleboro and Salem (New Jersey).[16] These autonomous bodies wanted legal, organizational self-determination in order to assemble freely and make their own decisions as African Methodists. They did not want their religious activities to be under European American control, but they did want their independent social space sanctioned by the larger society. The ability to function with reasonable assurance of autonomy could be secured only within the context of U.S. laws and regulations. Bethel Church of Philadelphia had already appealed to Pennsylvania courts for such legal rights; the courts had decided in favor of the congregation and established statutory precedents for independent African Methodism.[17]

Bethel Church called the organizing meeting in April 1816; the attending leaders committed themselves to forming an independent "connection"—a national, if not international, linkage of local congregations subscribing to, and organized under authority of, the beliefs and modes of governance of the *Methodist Book of Discipline*. The polity, or structure of governance, was an Episcopal hierarchy wherein bishops were the top ministerial authority, responsible for assigning clergy to congregations. The General Conference, a legislative body of ministerial representatives elected from geographic groupings of member congregations, made nonclerical decisions. The General Conference elected bishops. Women were not included in any of these arrangements.

Sixteen representatives from congregations in five mid-Atlantic cities attended the Philadelphia meeting, held on April 9, 1816. Although no women represented congregations, there were women at the meeting. Sarah Allen was there. She had been born a slave in 1764 in Isle of Wright County in Virginia and had been brought to the free territory of Philadelphia at age eight in order to live a less burdened life. In 1800 she married Richard Allen and accompanied him in his ministry. Sarah served as hostess for the 1816 conference at Bethel Church, thereby fulfilling the social expectations of the wife of the pastor of the host church.

Though no records place Doritha Hill at the April 9 meeting, there is strong evidence for her attendance. She was known as "Mother Hill" at Bethel Church of Baltimore, while her husband was a leading member of the society. He attended the 1816 meeting that organized the denomination, and it would have been normal, acceptable, and feasible for Doritha, as his wife, to accompany him. The presence of women at the Philadelphia meeting not only garnered to their gender more of the traditional authority associated with origination of the denomination but resulted in the earliest development of a gender-specific organization. Although there was no conscious attempt to challenge the formal authority of men, AME women already perceived their exclusion and were in a position to correct the situation. Their organization would survive beyond 1816 to become an important link in their acquisition of all denominational sources of power and in the eventual changes in Church structure to include women.

The Philadelphia meeting established an African Methodist Connection, accepting without change the polity and tenets of the white Methodist Episcopal Church. On April 11, 1816, the newly formed connection elected and consecrated Richard Allen as bishop, the first African American bishop in the United States. The AME Church was officially created, an ecclesiastic association was established, and the *Book of Discipline of the AME Church* outlined the formal positions of authority.[18] Occupants of these positions were authorized to make decisions and exercise power in the name of the larger body. The structure was composed of four units; specifications for three of the four were described in the *Discipline*—the Conference system, the order of ministry, and the laity. The fourth unit, the administration, was created later in the century as the denomination's membership expanded and created a need for more elaborate management.

The 1816 assembly had no disagreement with structural or religious tenets of Wesleyan Methodist tradition, though each congregation had grievances against the racist practices and some culture-specific worship practices of white churches in their cities. African Americans felt they understood the behavioral mandates of Christian theology better than white believers did because blacks endured the inhumane and discriminatory treatment of white Christians. African Americans would not merely preach Christianity but would be, by the absence of racial discrimination in their churches, living testimonies to the true mandates of their faith.[19] Women shared this understanding, though they were not part of the organizational arrangements adopted by the AME Church. However, they went on to carve positions for themselves within this structure.

STRUCTURE OF INDEPENDENCE

It is impossible to discuss issues of women, power, and structural change without first clarifying the organizational arrangement of the denomination. As noted above, there were three nineteenth-century structural divisions of African Methodism:

The *Ministry*, which was rigid in its prohibition against women's participation;

The *Conference system*, which seriously restricted women's authorized activity but allowed them to function outside the formal structure; and

The *Laity*, where AME women had a modicum of formal space in which to participate in organizational arrangements of their church.

Unlike in the Free African Society, women were not equal members in the structure adopted from European Americans. Though women were present at the meeting in 1816, there is no indication that they were allowed in the rooms where official discussions occurred. As African Americans adopted the Methodist polity for their new denomination, they made no provisions to include women. Women had to reshape the organizational domain, and to do so they needed to master the structural arrangements. It was a formidable task for an uneducated group socially relegated to second-class, if not third-class, status. There was a multitude of overlapping organizational layers of function and responsibility, and there were no eighteenth- or nineteenth-century models of women as visible and active partners in organizational arrangements. But it was a complex that was tacitly sanctioned by the larger U.S. political, governmental, and economic order. African Methodists were determined to be respected members of the society and the conference system—the order of ministry and laity of Methodist polity were sufficiently respectable for achieving their goal.

Women began to learn the new structure through their work in local congregations. These community-based bodies, sometimes numbering no more than eight to fifteen members, were part of the conference system, wherein elected delegates attended annual meetings of congregational groupings aligned on geographic lines. The groups, called "conferences," were authorized to govern and adjudicate the denominational activities of member congregations. Women began acquiring knowledge about Church polity within the congregational system and as such, began contesting for structural participation in the larger body.

Conferences

The conference system was complex and hierarchical; it functioned at the local, state, district, and national levels. At each conference meeting, elected delegates determined the spiritual and social programs in which local congregations would be required to participate. Conferences prescribed educational requirements for clergy, evaluated the moral character of ministers, assessed and collected funds from each minister and congregation in the conference, and oversaw expenditures. In case of conflict or unresolved disagreement, the next-higher conference served as the first arena of adjudication.

The highest of the decision-making assemblies was the General Conference; the Annual Conference was second, followed by the Quarterly Conference and then the Church Conference. Church Conferences were exclusively responsible for single congregations; they were to monitor and manage the process of their members toward goals set by the convening bishops of the next-higher conferences. Each congregation was required to hold a Church Conference four times a year—the pastor presided and women members were voting participants at this level.

Issues and grievances unresolved by pastors at these meetings were taken to the Quarterly or Annual Conference, where a presiding elder or bishop, respectively, was in charge. Quarterly Conferences monitored and managed a small cluster of Church Conferences and their congregations, while Annual Conferences were responsible for several Quarterly Conferences and their congregations. The Annual Conference body also decided on the distribution of material and ministerial resources in years when quadrennial General Conferences were not held.

The General Conference was the national, legislative body of African Methodism and comprised proportionally elected representatives from conferences below it. Whereas women could be and were delegates from arenas of work in the laity of a specific conference, they were not authorized to enter the ministry and therefore could not be elected to a voting position at any organizational level higher than the local Church Conference.

The General Conference meeting was responsible for developing policies for the denomination and designating how such policies would be implemented. Bishops of geographic areas were responsible for supervising the implementation of General Conference decisions. These men served for life and were elected by that national body. The General Conference held extensive authority over denominational life, but it could not change the "articles of religion, the episcopacy, members' privilege of trial and appeal, or general rules of the denomination."[20]

Ministry

As prescribed in the *Methodist Book of Discipline,* the ministry was the structural unit of the clergy, and ordination was the main prerequisite for entrance. Throughout the nineteenth century, women were strictly prohibited from ordination and by extension, the ministry. Prohibitions, even legal ones, however, do not always mean an absence of action; *Discipline* prohibitions did not prevent determined AME women from serving the functions of ministry. The prohibitions merely meant that women were not formally authorized to assume ministerial positions. Indeed, a variety of Church groups accepted AME women's ministerial services; we shall return to this point.

Like all entities that subscribed to Methodist polity, the AME Church vested power and authority in a ministry whose foundation was based on *itinerancy*, the understanding that individual ministers were periodically to be rotated among congregations rather than spending a lifetime with one local group. The itinerancy concept also included clusters, or "circuits," of congregations served by single pastoral ministers. One purpose of the circuit was to provide ministerial coverage to congregations in close proximity whose individual memberships were too small to support full-time pastors. Bishops responsible for Annual Conferences assigned ministers to circuits and single congregations. The six positions of the ministerial hierarchy, in ascending order, were: preacher, deacon, elder, pastor, presiding elder, and bishop. Ordination was required for all.

The position of bishop was also itinerant. Bishops, elected by the General Conference, constituted a Council of Bishops, responsible for rotating its members' assignments to geographic districts. Although their conference districts rotated, bishops served in the episcopacy for life. Itinerancy of AME ministers remained a distinguishing aspect of the Church throughout the nineteenth century and continues today.

Laity

The laity of the denomination was composed of all members of a local congregation; it was made up of small working groups that accomplished the actual enterprise of Methodism. Activities of the groups included, but were not limited to, conducting Sunday school classes, administering singing and praying bands, arranging for the cleaning and decoration of Church sanctuaries, conducting Bible study for children as well as adults, and other fundamental tasks that sustained the life of a congregation. Without members who carried out these functions, neither the local church nor the denomination could exist. The work and positions within the laity did not reflect the rigid hierarchy that characterized the ministry and conference structures. Nor was the laity dependent on ministerial authority. At local levels, getting work done was more important than adhering to formal authority bounded in the all-male hierarchy. Competence and participation were the appropriate criteria for identifying individuals who gave their services to local congregations.

Relationships within the laity were face to face, primary interactions, and they operated without much direct supervision from formal denominational authorities. This flexibility offered the organizational space women needed to learn how their Church functioned in structure and practice. The laity also provided an arena in which women could challenge the hierarchy and find ways to implement the individual and collective wills of women. The earliest successes at making structural changes to accommodate women would occur in the laity.

From these structural arrangements, an international Methodist denomination was forged by the hard work, commitment, and tenacity of African American women and men. More importantly, from deep within these configurations AME women began accumulating power that would give them a voice in their Church.

NOTES

1. See Owen D. Pelt and Ralph Lee Smith, *The Story of the National Baptists* (New York: Vantage, 1960), as well as James Washington, "Black Church History" class lecture (New York: Union Theological Seminary, September 1982).

2. Charles Wesley, *Richard Allen, Apostle of Freedom* (Washington, D.C.: Associated, 1935).

3. Albert J. Raboteau, *Slave Religion: The "Invisible" Institution in the South* (New York: Oxford University Press, 1978).

4. See Mechal Sobel, *Trabelin' On: The Slave Journey to an Afro-Baptist Faith* (Princeton, N.J.: Princeton University Press, 1988).

5. There were two periods of U.S. colonial history, during the eighteenth century, when Christian missionaries and evangelists were particularly active and successful in converting colonists to the faith. These periods of great Christian enthusiasm are referred to as "The Great Awaking" and the "Second Great Awakening."

6. For examples of early conversion testimonies see, Clifton H. Johnson, ed., *God Struck Me Dead* (Philadelphia: Pilgrim, 1964).

7. Wesley, *Richard Allen,* 77.

8. Jacqueline Jones, *Labor of Love, Labor of Sorrow: Black Women Work and the Family from Slavery to the Present* (New York: Vantage, 1986).

9. Wesley, *Richard Allen,* 77.

10. Wesley, *Richard Allen,* 77.

11. Class Leader's Book of Members of the Bethel African Methodist Episcopal Church (Baltimore: n.p., 1852), 16.

12. Joseph S. Thompson, *Bethel Gleanings* (Philadelphia: Robert S. Holland, 1881), 25; Richard R. Wright, African Methodist Episcopal Church, *Centennial Historical Souvenir of "Mother" Bethel A.M.E. Church* (Philadelphia: AME Book Concern, 1916), 34; Wesley, *Richard Allen,* 136; George A. Singleton, *The Romance of African Methodism: A Study of the African Methodist Episcopal Church* (New York: Exposition, 1952), 18; Maxwell Whiteman, *Articles of Association of the African Methodist Episcopal Church of the City of Philadelphia in the Commonwealth of Pennsylvania* (Philadelphia: Rhestoric, 1969), 14.

13. African Methodist Episcopal Church, *Class Leader's Book of Members of the Bethel African Methodist Episcopal Church* (Baltimore: n.p., 1852), 16.

14. Thompson, *Bethel Gleanings,* 25; Wright, AME Church, *Centennial Historical Souvenir,* 34; Wesley, *Richard Allen,* 136; Singleton, *Romance,* 18; Whiteman, *Articles.*

15. Max Weber in 1949 offered a typology of power, with traditional authority being one of them. Paul M. Harrison, *Authority and Power in the Free Church Tradition* (Princeton, N.J.: Princeton University Press, 1959), was a groundbreaking investigation of Weber's typology within a Protestant denomination.

16. Daniel Payne, *History of the African Methodist Episcopal Church* (Nashville, Tenn.: African Methodist Sunday School Union, 1891), 13.

17. Wesley, *Richard Allen,* 88–89, 148–49.

18. Wesley, *Richard Allen,* 155.

19. The idea that early African American Christians were committed to a "lived theology," as opposed to the systematic theology discussed and taught by white citizens, was derived from lecture presentations of Dr. James Washington during his course offering at Union Theological Seminary. See his "Black Church History."

20. Richard R. Wright, *The Negro in Pennsylvania: A Study in Economic History* (Philadelphia: AME Book Concern, n.d.)

2

✝

Building a Critical Mass

All laypeople as well as clergy members were expected to act in accordance with decisions of persons holding Church positions, and to adhere to policies regarding governance. Those in the hierarchy were expected to make decisions that not only agreed with Church tenets and policy, but did not cause significant losses of lay membership. A denomination cannot exist if its laity is not stable. It follows that numerical representation was a critical element in the ability of nineteenth-century women to cause structural changes. Their challenge was to bring enough women into the ranks to cause the all-male hierarchy to realize that the loss of the Church's women might mean the destruction of the entire denomination. Numbers are an important source of power, and AME women achieved a critical membership "mass."

In 1820 and 1830, there were 103.4 and 100.3 African American women for every hundred men, respectively.[1] It is no surprise that women also represented a majority of membership in African Methodist congregations. At its organization in 1816, the Church consisted of approximately 4,528 members in four locations. The women who attended that first meeting in Philadelphia represented their sisters in congregations of these cities, even though the conference gave them no official recognition. Historical records show that women were present in these first congregations but make no mention of the exact numbers. For example, we know

Table 2.1   AME Congregations of 1816

Distribution Ranked by Membership

Philadelphia, Pennsylvania	3,311
Baltimore, Maryland	1,066
Salem, New Jersey	110
Attleborough, Pennsylvania	41
Total	**4,528**

Source: Daniel A. Payne, *History of the African Methodist Episcopal Church* (Nashville, Tenn.: African Methodist Sunday School Union, 1891), 13.

that Doritha Hill, Annie Dickerson, and Mary A. Prout were active members in the 1816 Baltimore congregation. Similarly, Sarah Allen, Mother Duncan, Wealthy Dorsey, Hattie Thomas, Mother Shepherd, and Jane Ann Murray were all members of Bethel Church in Philadelphia. What is unclear is how many other women were members of these congregations, and what percentage of the total they represented. There are no records that present the gender distribution of this membership but table 2.1 does reflect the aggregate membership by location.

The inaugural meeting was followed in 1818 by a second meeting, again in Philadelphia. This time additional congregations—from New Jersey, Pennsylvania, and South Carolina—were admitted into the connectional body. The congregation from Charleston had the largest membership; overall, the denomination now had 6,757 members, in sixteen locations. The first volume of the official Church history supports the assertion that at this embryonic stage women accounted for the majority of local members,[2] a situation that represented a source of women's power and gave them a potential leadership role in the Church. In 1818 there was no true denomination, just a collection of small congregations that collectively represented less than 5 percent of the total black U.S. population. Consequently, all African Methodists focused on expanding the Church's presence across the new United States of America.

DOMESTIC EXPANSION

For the most, African Methodism had its foundations among free black populations of the mid-Atlantic coastal regions, particularly urban areas. Philadelphia, Baltimore, and Trenton, New Jersey,

Table 2.2   AME Congregations in 1818

Location	Number of Members
Philadelphia, Pennsylvania	3,311
Charleston, South Carolina	1,848
Baltimore, Maryland	1,066
Salem, New Jersey	110
Trenton, New Jersey	73
Snow Hill, Maryland	56
Westchester, Pennsylvania	46
Attleborough, Pennsylvania	41
Brunswick, New Jersey	40
Princeton, New Jersey	33
New Hope, New Jersey	29
Whitemarsh, Pennsylvania	29
Frankfort	28
Plemeth	8
Bridgeport	62
Total	**6,757**

Source: Daniel A. Payne, *The Semi-Centenary and the Retrospection of the African Methodist Episcopal Church in the United States* (Baltimore: Sherwood, 1866), 26–27.

were the more active early sites. When in 1818 the Charleston congregation joined, the Church had begun to extend its geographic presence (see table 2.2). After 1816, growth occurred beyond the core urban centers, deeper into mid-Atlantic states as well as in nearby states and territories. Women were favored in the general populations of these areas and were statistically more likely to constitute the numerical majorities of new congregations that were established.

For example, the census count of 1820 indicates that there were some 1,771,656 African Americans of all classes and statuses living in the states and territories that formed the United States. Of that number, 233,634 were free blacks and 1.5 million were enslaved, with female majorities in both groups. In his *The Free Black in Urban America: 1800–1850*, Leonard P. Curry reports that between 1790 and 1860 there were more African American women than men in fourteen cities (St. Louis was an exception). By 1820, there were 1.07 urban free black women to each man in the national population; in the fifteen cities Curry investigated, there were on average 1.29 women to every man. African American women held numerical sway within the general free black population from which African Methodism drew its members in these early years.[3]

At each of the Annual and General Conference meetings between 1816 and 1830, delegates authorized systematic expansion of the denomination into new areas of the mid-Atlantic—Washington, D.C., and nearby Georgetown, the Eastern Shore of Maryland, the regions of Harrisburg and Pittsburgh, and areas near Piscataway, New Jersey. Expansion was also to include "the country west of the Allegheny Mountains."[4] In each of these areas, women accounted for the majority of the free African American populations. The statistical likelihood of women representing numerical majorities in local congregations continued.[5] The 1820 Mott and Bridge Streets congregations of New York City are among the examples.

The first volume of authorized denominational history reports that in 1820 the membership of New York's Mott Street congregation "amounted to 20 souls, the majority of whom were women." In that same year, membership in the Bridge Street Church of Brooklyn stood at one hundred, and here too women were the majority. In Washington, D.C., at Union Bethel, more than half of the organizing members were women. At St. James in New Orleans—organized during this period though outside the mid-Atlantic area—63 percent of the persons who started the congregation were women.[6] There is no reason to assume that women were any less well represented in any of the other early churches.

In a similar fashion, women held majority status in the AME Church of Charleston, South Carolina. That congregation had the second-largest membership in the connectional body, accounting for just under one-fourth of the total 1820 membership. The Charleston Church merits special attention also because its fate had long-term consequences for the denomination. In 1820 there were 1.5 million enslaved African Americans among the total 1,771,656 total black population of the United States. More than 90 percent of these bonded persons lived in the country's southern, slaveholding region; 57 percent even of the free black population resided in southern states.[7] Therefore, when the Charleston congregation joined the denomination, the greatest potential for AME growth seemed to be in the South. But events of 1822 saw the demise of this congregation, as well as the thwarting of significant AME southern expansion.

In 1822 Denmark Vessey, a freed slave from the British West Indies who lived in the Charleston area, led a carefully planned insurrection. His elaborate plans were crushed before they could be implemented; "at least 139 black persons were arrested," and some forty-seven others were condemned to death for their participation.[8] The complexity and ingenuity of the rebels' plan terrified slave owners as well as most other southern whites. They were convinced that the continued presence of a northern-based, independent organization, even a Christian one, would incite new and even more potent disturbances.

Though some of Vessey's assistants were reported to have been free black members of the AME congregation of Charleston, no evidence linked the local Church itself to insurrection activities. Nevertheless, the Church was ordered disbanded, and southern states immediately enacted Black Codes to control the movement of all African Americans in slaveholding territories. The codes also prohibited free African Americans from entering certain areas of the South.[9] In this single series of actions by whites, the young denomination lost nearly two thousand of its members, its strongest presence in the South, and unrestricted access to the largest population of African Americans in the nation. This was a major loss.

In Maryland, however, though it was a border state where Black Codes severely hampered the itinerant and evangelizing activities of clergy from the Baltimore AME congregation, the work was not terminated. This founding congregation of the denomination proceeded to organize three new societies before the Civil War began in 1861; women were directly responsible for much of the expansion. Individuals like Annie Dickerson and Mary A. Prout continued to be active for the local body as well as for the new denomination as a whole. Zilpha Elaw was another who would not be intimidated by Black Code restrictions. She recorded her activities in an autobiography published in 1846. Zilpha, a preaching woman of the 1830s, described attending a Baltimore Annual Conference meeting with other ministers of the "colored denomination." She left the gathering and proceeded to hold prayer meetings throughout Maryland, in direct defiance of travel restrictions.[10]

Such bravery in this era was clearly due to women's knowledge that the black community needed strong and stable social organizations to struggle against slavery and racial injustice, and for their rights as humans. Women also knew that the economic and social strength garnered by individual African Americans was both small and highly unstable; it could be eradicated within minutes by the forces of racism that pervaded the country. If blacks were to survive and perpetuate themselves as a people, they needed social organizations—organizations that linked individual strengths and resources into a collective power that would directly and indirectly benefit everyone in the community. This was not a new idea. Its roots were in the African heritage of the community and had already been used successfully by enslaved African Americans seeking freedom on the "Underground Railroad." To build critical social structures and enhance the survival of a people, AME women were willing to confront restrictions of the southern Black Code; in the process they epitomized a distinctive African American feminism. Historians Filomina Steady and Rosalyn Terborg-Penn discuss this feminism in the context of women's organizing through survival networks like the AME Church. Zilpha Elaw and women like her demonstrated this black feminism during the antebellum period of the nineteenth century.[11]

The centrality of community was equally present in AME women's commitment to building the denomination. They were intent on creating a religious and social organization that would give moral underpinnings to the daily lives of individuals who constituted the African American community. They would build an independent association that could be an advocate for their people, who were still deprived of human rights as well as of social, political, and economic opportunities; who were yet despised because of their birth; and who were still disenfranchised in a society built on their labor. Such an independent social organization could also oppose the system of slavery that held millions of black people in bondage. Their denomination would provide a political voice for all African Americans. Those who challenged the southern Black Codes steadily applied themselves to this work.

African Methodist women of the 1820s believed that in addition to its religious intent, the social and moral mission of their denomination made it an organizational tradition that could meet many needs of their community. As such, they gave priority to building and strengthening it. When Black Codes interfered with southern organizing, women like Zilpha Elaw eagerly planted churches beyond the Allegheny Mountains and in other new territories of the United States. For example, a New York Annual Conference was established in 1822, and in 1824 a Cincinnati group joined the connection. The Cincinnati experience stands out, because it demonstrates both the women's commitment to creating religious organizations and the importance of women's numbers in the larger equation of changing Church structures.

Between 1815 and 1824, there was a majority of women among the 337 African Americans of Cincinnati. This black community had always envisioned independent Christian worship, and among its members were a number committed to the Methodist tradition. Women numbered forty within the seventy-three African Americans led in worship by ministers from the white Methodist Episcopal Church. Some of this smaller group wanted independent worship, but all kept their relationship with the white denomination. However, members of that Methodist body fiercely discriminated against black leaders at an 1823 camp meeting and enough was enough.[12]

The African Methodists authorized a committee to deliberate on the situation and to determine what should be done; there were three women in this decision-making body. The committee decided for independence, the resolution was sustained, and the Cincinnati church was received into the AME connection on February 4, 1824.[13] Here again, most members of the local congregation were women, as were most of the decision makers who chose independence and African Methodist affiliation.

We cannot overlook these exemplary activities of black women, not merely because their presence was critical to development and stability of the Church, but because their activities illustrate aspects of nineteenth-century African American feminism (though they would probably not be termed "radical" or "feminist" by today's Euro-American definitions). The AME women were focused on constructing an independent social organization that would strengthen the African American community of Cincinnati; gender equity was probably not among their first priorities. Their behavior arose from a cultural ethos deeply rooted in their African heritage. Strong community was understood to produce strong individuals, and strong individuals were expected to participate in the full life of the community, to keep it strong. Women were among those who organized the Ohio church because it was the action culturally consistent with African Americans' understandings of community, work, and individual participation.

Women also contributed to the formation of the Western Annual Conference in 1830. The new conference encompassed all local congregations and missionary activities west of the Allegheny Mountains, an area that by 1833 reported 1,131 members and twenty-four churches between Pittsburgh and the western border of Ohio. These new members added to acquisitions of 1822 in the New York Annual Conference, as well as to the 1824 growth in Cincinnati. The new accessions were concurrent with nominal increases in conferences that had originated the denomination. However, though growth in Ohio and New York reported at the 1836 General Conference represented substantial development, it barely offset the 1822 loss of the Charleston church. Still, the AME Church would not be daunted by the losses or by the Black Codes. As if to reinforce their determination, the 1844 General Conference was held in Baltimore, a slaveholding state. Now there were four Annual Conferences and 11,059 members (see table 2.3).

One significant aspect of the earliest expansion of African Methodism was that women formed the majorities of the new congregations' memberships, and they maintained this numerical strength as expansion went beyond the Allegheny Mountains into territories that eventually became the states of Ohio, Illinois, Indiana, and parts of Missouri. In 1840 the total free black population in that area stood at 6,459, largely due to the number of African Americans migrating to new regions in a continuing search for refuge from enslavement and racial oppression.[14] Escaped slaves had run away to

Table 2.3   1836–1840 Distribution of Members by Annual Conference

Year	Ohio/Western	Philadelphia	Baltimore	New York	Total
1836	1,131	3,344	2,052	743	7,270
1837	1,507	3,443	2,345	810	8,105
1838	1,817	4,044	2,794	1,053	9,708
1839	NR	4,479	2,300	1,222	8,001
1840	2,488	4,659	2,636	1,276	11,059

Source: Payne, *History of the African Methodist Episcopal Church*, 125–32.
Note: Data for 1840 was reported at the 1844 General Conference in Baltimore.

the western territories and many ex-slaves had been brought there and freed by philanthropic masters. Women represented a majority of the total population in the territories as well as of the ex-slaves brought and freed by white masters. African American women and their mulatto offspring benefited from these relocations, and the AME Church became the congregational choice of many.

Delegates to the 1840 General Conference truly had not expected so many new members from beyond the Allegheny Mountains when they assigned a missionary to the region. However, when delegates gathered for the next quadrennial assembly, in 1844, they were staggered by statistics from the West: there were two thousand new members, seventy-two congregations, and forty-seven church buildings in Indiana and Illinois. Women steadfastly led the formation of new congregations in these territories and continued to account for the majority of their members.

African Methodism continued to expand in regions that would become Ohio. Its activities revolved around Cincinnati, where a second congregation was organized in 1840. This new church called itself Brown's Chapel AME; sixteen of its twenty-six original members were women.[15] Local churches were also established in slaveholding states of Kentucky and Missouri, with 150 new members reported in the latter. The situation in St. Louis, Missouri, deserves examination as it illustrates additional ways in which women were involved in this successful expansion.

Pricilla Baltimore prepared the way in St. Louis. She was not only the assigned itinerant minister but single-handedly laid foundations for African Methodism in this area of the Mississippi River Valley. She had been born a slave (her master being her father) in Bourbon County, Kentucky, on May 13, 1801. She had been converted to Christianity and Methodism by Bishop Hendrick of the white Methodist Episcopal Church. She was later purchased for $1,100 by a missionary who allowed her to buy her freedom; Priscilla accomplished this goal in seven years. She was known for her hard work, honesty, and Christian commitment. On more than one occasion she operated a ferry, carrying passengers on her barge across the Mississippi River from East St. Louis, Illinois, to St. Louis, Missouri.

In 1840, when an AME minister was assigned to missionary work in the Missouri-Kentucky-Illinois area, Priscilla became well known to him. On several occasions he was a passenger on her ferry and often found accommodations with her when his work required an overnight stay. Significantly, Priscilla Baltimore's reputation among white slaveholders was so favorable that she was able to bring entire congregations of enslaved persons to hear the AME minister preach. When worship services ended, Priscilla ferried her passengers back across the river without incident. On one occasion, she brought some three hundred enslaved African Americans from Missouri to Illinois to attend such a service.[16]

When the Official Board of the new AME congregation needed a place to hold its first meeting in 1841, it is no surprise that it used Priscilla Baltimore's home, though a Louisa Carter was listed as the Church's first member. The missionary assigned by the denomination carried official authority and Louisa Carter was first on the membership roll, but it was Priscilla Baltimore who brought the idea of African Methodism to the largest number of potential members. Without her, the denomination's success in the St. Louis area would never have occurred.

By their individual personalities and their numerical presence, women were equally central to developments in Illinois. In 1846, there were seven women in a group of ten persons who organized the local church of Bloomington, Illinois. A small group, including women, of the three hundred African Americans in Chicago began holding prayer meetings as early as 1844. When their numbers grew, they moved to the home of Maria Parker. The prayer group officially united with the AME Church in 1847; five of its seven charter members were women. This was the Quinn Chapel AME Church, which was to be the denomination's flagship congregation of Chicago. Among its first members were Rachel Day, Matilda Lucas, Mary Jane Randall, A. T. Hall, and Maria More.[17] When the first Methodist class of Quinn Chapel was organized, eight of the ten members were women.[18]

Quinn Chapel was also known for its active fight to abolish the institution of slavery, as well as for its assistance to runaway slaves. Four women, most likely original members of the congregation, are reputed to have been "conductors" on the Underground Railroad, which brought runaways out of the South and into free territories. These women's success in such activities earned them the distinctive nickname, "The Big Four."

When the men of the East gathered for the 1844 General Conference, we can be sure they would have been even more astonished at the explosion of western membership if they had appreciated how indispensable women had been for increases in the area. In fact, women—who continually contributed to the formation of churches and were in the majority in local congregations—were forbidden ordination into AME clergy, could hold no official position in the Church polity, could not vote on denominational affairs, and only rarely received official recognition for their efforts and accomplishments.[19]

But there was one man who was conscious of women's pivotal contribution and wrote about it. Benjamin Tucker Tanner, a prominent bishop of the early Church, argued that any itinerant missionary of this period would gladly testify to the indispensability of women. Missionaries, he declared, would affirm that women promoted AME expansion under the most difficult circumstances. In his history of early Church development, Tanner suggested that a typical reminiscence of a missionary would read: "I came to this sister's house, and I was hungry, and she fed me, dividing even the last loaf; my feet were cold, well nigh frosted, she administered to me; to keep me comfortable at night, she and husband forsook their only bed; and when morning came, the very best that their scanty larder could afford, was given to me."[20]

Tanner's recognition is noteworthy not only because it was rare but because it supports our understanding that women's early activities achieved a historical reputation for themselves as well as accumulated membership numbers for the denomination.

Numbers are an essential prerequisite to power; without a "critical mass," it is difficult to convert the potential represented by organization and resources into actual ability to create change. Women accounted for some 60 percent (9,712 of 16,190 members) of the 1846 African Methodist Episcopal Church, in which there were 198 local congregations.[21] Their numerical strength was the epicenter of AME growth and a critical indicator of the power in Church decision making that they were gathering.

During the pre–Civil War period, territories west of the Mississippi River also experienced the coming of African Methodism, and again, women were crucial. Gold was discovered in 1848 in the Sacramento, California, area. Enslaved and free African Americans migrated to California partly by their masters' decisions, partly in search of riches, and partly in search of a place free of racism. In 1852, Mrs. Edward Gomez envisioned a San

Francisco community of African Americans that would offer the
stability and moral foundations of organized religion.

Living in New York City, before her travel west, Mrs. Gomez
knew the AME missionary who would later appear in San Francisco. In California, she received him as a welcome addition to
the growing African American community, as there was little
spiritual focus to the organized social life in the area. Any existing cohesion was more a result of reaction to crime and vice than
of positive moral influence on behavior. Mrs. Gomez, giving priority to the needs of her community, opened her home to the
African Methodist minister. On a memorable Sunday in February 1852, a prayer meeting was held in her home, and Union
Bethel AME Church of San Francisco began.[22] Like other AME
women, Mrs. Gomez reflected the community-centered ethos of
nineteenth-century African American feminism.

In southern California, Biddy Mason was the pivotal link in organizing African Methodism. She too envisioned an independent,
self-sufficient, and cohesive African American community, in this
case in Los Angeles. She had been brought to the West by her Mississippi slave master and had been freed in California in 1856. No
records show that she ever had a husband; most indications are
that her three children were those of her master. In Mississippi,
Ms. Mason had been trained as a midwife, a profession that provided her with economic stability in Los Angeles. After her man-
umission, she delivered most of the babies born in the city between 1851 and 1886, earned $2.50 a day. By as early as 1866,
Biddy Mason had saved enough money to purchase the first of
several pieces of real estate.[23] In 1872, Biddy Mason's home on
Spring Street was the site of the first AME congregation in Los
Angeles. Her family is listed as one of nine "prominent" African
American families that inaugurated the local church.[24]

In 1888, a small group of Californians in Pasadena established
a congregation in which women represented at least half of the
membership. In Houston, Texas, in 1875, six of the seven persons
who pioneered Wesley Chapel AME Church were women.[25] These
instances demonstrate that women in this period maintained their
roles as organizers of local congregations and as charter members
of those churches, and that they continued to form the majorities
in their memberships.

Before the Civil War, as the denomination expanded across the continent, the vast majority of African Americans still lived in southern states and in subjugation. The Emancipation Proclamation of 1862 brought the AME Church an opportunity to open a virtual treasure chest of new members. Even before the end of the war, the Church rushed to bring its message to the freed African American population in the South, and denominational leaders immediately entered institutional relationships with agencies of the federal government.

On April 27, 1863, a white minister who was a financial officer of the Freedmen's Aid Association brought a petition to the Baltimore Annual Conference. He asked the assembly to assign two preachers "as missionaries to care for the moral, social and religious interest of the freedmen of South Carolina who were . . . left . . . by their former white pastors, who had fled before the advancing and conquering army of the Union."[26] The conference agreed, and a direct linkage was thus created between AME ministers who traveled with Northern forces and the liberation of African Americans from slavery. It was a complex relationship. The African Methodists were directly attached to the Federal army. In addition, they brought the newly emancipated women and men a message of Christian faith, deliverance, and salvation. The black military also represented the strongest and most visible African American social organization in the United States. The ministers were inviting their recently freed sisters and brothers to join this independent black denomination. This message of multiple identities was a powerful one, with great collective as well as personal potential.

This was the first opportunity for the southerners to belong to a national organization committed to the advancement of African people; to be subjected no longer to white supervision and authority; to disassociate themselves from white organizations that were responsible for their enslavement. It was an opportunity to be collectively self-determining. Entire congregations of recently emancipated women and men became African Methodists; they used buildings left to them by fleeing white southerners and seized by Northern armies.[27] This was a wholly new and different method of Church expansion, but women were no less visible and active in these southern congregations than in the North and West, and their numerical superiority did not slip.

Just as in the northern states and western territories, women became the most important numerical bloc in the thirteen states that constituted the Confederacy. This was clearly the case for four typical cities where African Methodism found large numbers of new members during and after the Civil War. Women accounted for 54 percent of the black population of Augusta, Georgia; 53 percent in Charleston, South Carolina; 51 percent in Nashville, Tennessee; and 54 percent of the African Americans in Norfolk, Virginia (see table 2.4).

Women were the numerical majority in these cities and in congregations that aligned with the AME Church. It was a gender distribution that existed in the denomination throughout the United States for the remainder of the century.

INTERNATIONAL EXPANSION

Domestic as well as international expansion was always an objective of Protestant denominations and the AME Church was no exception. As early as 1827, its international activities focused on Haiti and Santo Domingo; Annual Conferences assigned ministers to these territories in the denomination's early years. The Baltimore conference so charged such ministers at that time and did so again in 1830, when eager volunteers came forward to work among descendants of Africans in the Caribbean. The success of the Haitian Revolution in 1804 had tapped the nationalistic fervor of African Methodists, and Baltimore responded to the enthusiasm of its ministers. By 1829, there were 182 members reported in Haiti. The 1840 General Conference reclaimed from Annual Conferences the authority to manage international missionary appointments.[28] Though there is no official record of the involvement of women in this international expansion, other evidence makes it hard to imagine African Methodism developing anywhere without women's presence and active participation.

More is known about the growth and termination of the Church in Canada, where there was a significant African American presence early in the nineteenth century. Although persons of African descent would surely have settled in Canada through normal economic and political processes, much of the growth of the Canadian black population was a direct result of slavery in the United States. An esti-

Table 2.4 Gender Distributions for Select States and Cities of Free Black and Enslaved Populations

| State | *Enslaved* | | *Free* | | |
& City	*Male*	*Female*	*Male*	*Female*	*TOTAL*
Georgia	229,193	233,005	1,669	1,831	465,698
Augusta	2,195	2,528	88	132	4,943
South Carolina	196,571	205,835	4,548	5,366	412,320
Charleston	10,245	10,915	711	1,233	23,104
Tennessee	136,370	139,349	3,538	3,762	283,019
Nashville	3,825	3,881	311	386	8,403
Virginia	249,438	241,382	27,712	30,321	548,853
Norfolk	2,492	2,665	588	912	6,657

Source: U.S. Census, 1864, 60–70, 447–52, 458–62, 506–19.

mated eleven hundred to two thousand women and men from Cincinnati, Ohio, had migrated to Canada by 1829. They were searching for new places to raise families and start communities, away from the racist and repressive restrictions that barred free blacks from the new Northwestern Territory of the United States.

The Fugitive Slave Act of 1850 was another factor influencing African American relocation to Canada. This legislation declared that even free blacks living in nonslaveholding states could be captured, or recaptured, and enslaved in the South. Thousands of African Americans fled to Canada rather than risk renewed persecution under this tyrannous legislation.[29]

Local congregations of Afro-Canadians joined with the U.S. AME Church as early as 1831, when 448 such members were listed in denominational documents. By 1850 the number had risen to 793, and by 1855 to two thousand. Despite this obvious growth, the cross-national affiliation lasted only twenty-four years. Differences in legal statutes, compounded by overwhelming differences in interpretations of the legal relationship between congregations and the denomination as a whole led to a severance. On September 29, 1856, in Chatham, Ontario, representatives from both groups of African Methodists amicably dissolved the relationship.

Although there is little information on the women who organized and helped create congregations in Canada, we know of one who was central to the separation. The group that negotiated the separation met in the home of a Mrs. Taylor. She resided in

Chatham and appears to have been the wife of Rev. Jeremiah Taylor, though we need to know more about her and other Canadian women of the tradition.

The very fact of women's numerical strength in the fabric of the AME Church is critical because of the potential for women to combine their numerical presence with the other two sources of power—organization and resources. Throughout the nineteenth century and in every geographic location, the future of the Church depended on building a critical membership mass. Women were that critical mass for African Methodism, a factor important in the evolving ability of women to bring gender changes to the Church. In the following chapters we turn to AME women and organization.

NOTES

1. E. Franklin Frazier, *The Negro Church in America* (New York: Schocken, 1949; reprint, New York: Schocken, 1963), 180–82.

2. Daniel A. Payne, *The Semi-Centenary and the Retrospection of the African Methodist Episcopal Church in the United States* (Baltimore: Sherwood, 1866); Benjamin Tucker Tanner, *An Outline of Our History and Government for African Methodist Churchmen* (Philadelphia: n.p., 1884).

3. Leonard P. Curry, *The Free Black in Urban America, 1800–1850: The Shadow of the Dream* (Chicago: University of Chicago Press, 1981), 253–54.

4. Daniel A. Payne, *History of the African Methodist Episcopal Church* (Nashville, Tenn.: African Methodist Sunday School Union, 1891), 21.

5. In Baltimore and Philadelphia, charter sites of African Methodism, there were 1.40 free black women for every 1.36 men. In New York, Brooklyn, Washington, Pittsburgh, and Charleston—cities into which the denomination would expand before 1830—there was a similar ratio of women to men. Curry, *The Free Black in Urban America.*

6. Payne, *History*, 35–6; Simms Family, "Register of Members of Union Bethel African Methodist Episcopal Church," manuscript journal, Simms Family Papers, box 1, Moorland-Spingarn Research Center, Howard University, Washington, D.C., 1839; John A. Thornton, "The History of St. James African Methodist Episcopal Church," in *A Century of African Methodism in the Deep South* (New Orleans: St. James AME Church, c. 1946), 75.

7. U.S. Census for 1820, Washington, D.C.

8. John Hope Franklin, *From Slavery to Freedom: A History of Negro Americans* (New York: Vintage, 1969), 212.

9. Franklin, *From Slavery to Freedom*, 222; Payne, *History*, 45.

10. Jarena Lee, *Religious Experience and Journal of Mrs. Jarena Lee: Giving an Account of Her Call to Preach the Gospel* (Philadelphia: n.p., 1849).

11. See Rosalyn Terborg-Penn, Sharon Harley, and Andrea Benton Rushing, *Women in Africa and the African Diaspora* (Washington, D.C.: Howard University Press, 1987), 3–24, 43–64.

12. David A Gerber, *Black Ohio and the Color Line, 1816–1915* (Chicago: University of Illinois Press, 1976), 14.

13. Benjamin W. Arnett, *Proceedings of the Semi-Centenary Celebration of the African Methodist Episcopal Church of Cincinnati* (Cincinnati: H. Watkin, 1874), 17, 29.

14. Peter M. Berwanger, *The Chronological History of the Negro in America* (New York: New American Library, 1969), 20; Leon Litwack, *North of Slavery: The Negro in the Free States, 1790–1860* (Chicago: University of Chicago Press, 1961).

15. Arnett, *Proceedings*, 56.

16. James A. Handy, *Scraps of African Methodist Episcopal History* (Philadelphia: AME Book Concern, n.d.), 345–46; Alexander Walker Wayman, *My Recollections of African Methodist Episcopal Minutes, or Forty Years' Experience in the African Methodist Episcopal Church* (Philadelphia: AME Book Rooms, 1882), 18; George A. Singleton, *The Romance of African Methodism: A Study of the African Methodist Episcopal Church* (New York: Exposition, 1952), 72–73; Richard R. Wright Jr., *The Encyclopaedia of the American Methodist Episcopal Church* (Philadelphia: AME Book Concern, 1947), 360.

17. Ashley B. Carter, "A Century of Christian Service," in *Quinn Chapel African Methodist Episcopal Church Centennial Celebration* (Chicago: n.p., 1947); John T. Jenifer, *Centennial Retrospect History of the African Methodist Episcopal Church* (Nashville, Tenn.: Sunday School Union, c. 1912), 34.

18. Ethel Payne, "City's 2 Oldest Churches Quinn 106—Olivet 92," *Chicago Defender*, February 14, 1953; Illinois Writers Project, "Churches: Organizations and Conventions," Vivian G. Harsh Collection of the Carter G. Woodson Branch, box 33, Chicago Public Library, Chicago, Illinois, 1940.

19. Benjamin Arnett, *The Budget* (unpublished, 1888), 169; Payne, *History*, 170.

20. Tanner, *Outline*, 136–37.

21. U.S. Census 293 supports the numerical majority of women and the stated relationships.

22. Amanda Berry Smith, *Amanda Smith: The Colored Evangelist* (Chicago: Christian Writers, 1921); L. L. Berry, *A Century of Missions of the African Methodist Episcopal Church*, 1840–1940 (New York: Gutenberg, 1942), 60–61; Wright, *Centennial Encyclopedia of the AME Church*.

23. N. F. Mendoza, *The Argonaut*, February 22, 1990, 12.

24. Mendoza, *The Argonaut*.

25. Wright, 461; *The Red Book of Houston: A Compendium of Social, Professional, Religious, Education and Industrial Interests of Houston's Colored Population* (Houston: Sotex, c. 1915), 75–76.

26. Payne, *History*, 467.

27. For discussions of the number of blacks that joined the AME Church and left white denominations, see Payne, *History*, 471–72; Harry V. Richardson, *Dark Salvation: The Story of Methodism as It Developed among Blacks in America* (New York: Anchor, 1976), 195; William Pope Harrison, *The Gospel among the Slaves: A Short Account of Missionary Operations among the African Slaves in the Southern States* (Nashville, Tenn.: Methodist Episcopal Church South, 1893), 318–24.

28. Payne, *History*, 106.

29. Litwack, *North of Slavery*, 7, 249.

3

✛

Organizing for Effectiveness

The citizens of the United States are well known for forming voluntary organizations to accomplish a wide array of goals and objectives. However, this does not mean that it is easy for them to agree on formal procedures. We find it even more difficult to concretize such behaviors in order to establish the formal organizations. Once established, such formal structures combine the forces derived from the size of their memberships and from the material and nonmaterial resources of the members. This is the force that makes organizations such strong social phenomena and critical factors in any consideration of power.

The "Daughters of Conference" was the first organization for AME women. Though not a true association at its beginnings, the Daughters of Conference set the pattern for how AME women would act collectively throughout the nineteenth century. It was the precursor of women's collective struggle to bring structural changes to the Church. The Daughters of Conference began in 1816, as the denomination itself was being formed. The women's grouping was the foundation on which three positions for women were created in the AME Church—stewardess, female evangelist, and deaconess.

The year 2000 saw a woman elected bishop of the Church—the culmination of AME women's nineteenth-century struggle for structural inclusion. This accomplishment ended most structural barriers that had kept women out of the hierarchy. In the 118 years it took to accomplish gender inclusiveness, women were steadfast in their struggle. They simultaneously grew in numbers, developed skills of organization, and generally gained strength to force the male leadership to make changes.

Women not only attended the founding conference of the AME Church but, at that time, began activities leading to the first of several women's associations—though creating such an organization was not the women's focus. As men began deliberating on the formation of an independent, connectional church, women gathered in a separate room at Mother Bethel Church in Philadelphia. Nineteenth-century daily life was separated into gender-specific spheres, so it was logical and correct for the two 1816 meetings to be separated. Women heartily supported the idea of an independent church and did not necessarily feel excluded from the formal proceedings. Rather, they gathered and began other important tasks necessary to realize the benefits expected to be gained from a religious association.

The entire black American community lived under the stigma and racial exclusion that white society placed on African Americans and their descendants. Few were respected for their worth as human beings or individuals, despite the fact that white America was being developed by the collective labor of blacks. Most African Americans accepted the United States as their permanent new home and searched for ways to become respectable parts of its social fiber. This quest for social respectability was particularly important among the free blacks and should be understood in the context of a "politics of respectability." The historian Evelyn Higginbotham has explored the significance of respectability in her study of Baptist women, and sociologist Cheryl Townsend Gilkes has extended this idea to include "elegance." Together, the conceptions incorporate African Americans' emphases on organization and public displays of elegance, an emphasis that became significant community-survival mechanisms. Aspirations toward social respectability, and the creation of distinctive cultural ethos, were internal aspects of community survival.[1]

The all-pervading pressures of economic, social, and political deprivation structured the conditions of daily life for blacks in the United States. White society attempted to push blackness and people of African heritage into invisibility. Blacks saw social organizations as effective weapons, vehicles for mustering the collective resources of the African American community to bring about improvement in its condition and to garner recognition—and some degree of respect—from the larger American society. The public presentation of an elegant self and group—that is, extraordinary attire, concern for outward appearance generally—was given priority as part of the quest for social respectability.

The organizers of the AME Church firmly believed that an independent black denomination would enhance the social respectability of African Americans and advance the community's aspirations for social mobility. In this context the community's representatives—its clergymen—needed to be "acceptable" in outward appearance, in fact as "elegant" as the community could collectively afford. Therefore, women at Mother Bethel Church in 1816 assumed responsibility for improving the appearance of the clergy. The women began repairing the clothing of the male delegates, thereby not only demonstrating support for the new church but providing the first harbinger of a women's organization.

It is not difficult to imagine Sarah Allen, Doritha Hill, and the others accompanying their clerical relatives to the historic meeting. They had traveled from Baltimore, Wilmington, Salem, and Attleborough. The roads were particularly muddy from the thawing snow and ice in that April of 1816, and housing, food, and other facilities were not readily available on the way. Even where such accommodations existed, there was never a guarantee that African Americans would be welcomed. Everyone arrived in Philadelphia tired and looking less than their best. Sarah Allen was the hostess for the seminal meeting at Mother Bethel. Unquestionably, she offered everyone food and accommodations in which to wash and refresh themselves. Doritha Hill certainly volunteered to help prepare and serve refreshments. By the time the men began their formal deliberations, the women had observed the men's torn coats, tattered shirts, missing buttons, and generally bedraggled appearance. It would not be tolerated. The women refused to permit the leaders of their community to be so shabby.

As the men discussed denominational affiliation in one room, the women gathered in another with coats, jackets, pants, shirts, and other clothing in need of repair. They began a campaign of mending, darning, stitching, and sewing. They knew that the delegates next door were among the wisest members of the African American community, and that as members of the clergy they were in the best position to represent black people publicly. The women intended to ensure that their clergy made the best physical impression the community's material means would allow. The women were participating in African American politics of respectability. That is, they were attending to the observable details by which white society seemed to judge whether or not blacks were a "civilized" people, ready to be accepted and respected as equals in the human family. The politics of respectability was assumed at the time to be an effective way to upgrade the quality of African American social life vis-à-vis white standards—though in the end, even the most ardent efforts would not achieve social acceptance by whites.

Nevertheless, at that historic moment in 1816, the women's actions were important in the formation of the new denomination. At the same time, they constituted an implicit protest of the exclusion of women from the Church's organizational domain. It was a latent challenge, but a challenge nonetheless. By this challenge, women asserted themselves into the men's deliberations, providing valued and needed services not attended to by other elements of the Church. They were making space for women's presence where no such space officially existed. Further, they were establishing a precedent for the face-to-face, gender-specific activities by which following generations would expand the place of women in African Methodist polity. Face-to-face activities also became organizational mechanisms for developing skills of community organizing. Such skills and experience would allow women to create more elaborately structured social arrangements, inside and outside of the Church.

There was no resistance to African American women's early organizational efforts. After all, women sitting together to darn and mend clothing represented acceptable cultural behavior, in both black and white communities. It posed no threat to the privileges accorded men, to men's priority rights to leadership, to the likely trajectory of church development, or to the overall patriarchal character of U.S. society. Other women took up the practice, doing similar work in support of the denomination, and the activity spread beyond the Philadelphia Conference to vicinities surrounding Baltimore. Women formed their groups independent of denominational meetings, wherever congregations existed or were being created. These Daughters of Conference groups became the original and benchmark grouping of AME women. They provided important experience in gathering in order to further goals, making collective decisions, abiding by group choices, and dividing labor in order to accomplish specified objectives. The Daughters of Conference was the model for future gender-specific, social arenas wherein women acquired skills in organizational management. Nothing else in the new denomination accommodated women's groups or their skills.

Women assumed responsibility for repairing garments, filling ministers' empty stomachs, providing itinerant preachers temporary housing, and attending to the general material well-being of the new church's clergy. Some ten years later, male delegates to the Annual Conference decided to express their appreciation of the women's work. They publicly thanked the Daughters of Conference for a financial contribution of $18.27 that helped support conference pastors. A year later, in 1828, the local groups were officially designated as the "Daughters of Conference."[2]

Thus the designation was an after-the-fact response to women's demonstrated success. Belated acknowledgment would become the common pattern; the Church's male hierarchy would consistently fail to respond proactively to the presence and initiatives of women. In the short run, the reactive pattern was an effective tactic, one that temporarily harnessed the women's growing power within the boundaries of male authority. In the long term, however, mere reaction proved unsuccessful; women's groups grew into an indispensable denominational infrastructure that not only gave needed support to the developing Church but challenged the error of excluding women from structural positions.

The Daughters of Conference was but one of the groups that constituted women's expanding network, which paralleled the exclusively male denominational structure. The network was informal but indispensable contribution to the functioning of the Church. Men held all official positions and thereby all official authority, but they did not always control the sources of power that undergirded their positions and authority. Men could not always assume that their will would be implemented. The network of women's groups,

in contrast, was outside the Church's formal arrangements and possessed no official authority. However, women, who accounted for
the majority of the denomination's members, learned to organize,
and through their associations acquired resources that the Church
needed if it was to continue to grow. The success of the denomination would depend on establishing a working relationship between
the all-male formal structure and the women who increasingly controlled the true sources of power.

During the formative years of 1816 to 1850, the relationship of
women to organizational sources of power was intimately bound
to expansion of the Church throughout the territories that became
the present-day United States. Their numerical strength in newly
established congregations increased, and so did their organizational activity. Daughters of Conference groups attracted new
members in New York, Massachusetts, Pennsylvania, Maryland,
the western territories of Ohio, and everywhere else that African
Methodism planted congregations. The groups became normal
parts of congregational life, though their raison d'être related to
the life of the larger denominational body. The minutes of the
1828 General Conference praised women's work, but in reality
the praise was an acknowledgment of the financial contributions
the Daughters of Conference made to support the clergy. This was
income from which each ordained pastor expected to receive a
portion. Despite this affirmation of women's growing indispensability, the Church's policy-making body did not incorporate
women's work into the structures, then or at any time in the antebellum period.

The Daughters of Conference was but one of several gender-
specific mutual-aid societies that were common among African
American communities during the eighteenth and nineteenth centuries. Indeed, the 1787 Free African Society, which gave birth to
African Methodism, was one such association. As the number of
local churches increased, women organized a variety of aid
groups with such names as the Independent Daughters of Hope,
United Daughters of Tapaico, Sisters of the Good Shepherd,
Daughters of Sharon, the African Female Tract Association, and
the Daughters of Samaria. The activities of such organizations
continued to provide funds, materials, and other resources that
added to the strength of the denomination. Such contributions

were vital in meeting the general operating expenses of local congregations as well as of the national assemblies. But the increasing numbers and success of the women's societies also brought difficulties and tensions.

On August 15, 1828, the antebellum newspaper *Freedom's Journal* published an editorial that was a (somewhat backhanded) testimony to the significance of the women's organizations. The editor was displeased with the increasing demand by women for public recognition of their organizational work. He wrote, "We are much in favor of all associations, whose immediate objects are to afford assistance to the sick and distressed. . . . We rejoice that they exist among us; but our duty to the community compels us once again to denounce such an uncommon sight as a female procession, dressed in the full costume of their order."[3] The editorial affirmed women's skills in creating aid groups and called these organizations important ingredients in the social infrastructure that safeguarded the general welfare of the African American community.

However, the editorial was also evidence of the determination of women to receive public notice. The AME Church had acknowledged the Daughters of Conference in denominational documents, but apparently other women's groups were omitted and did not appreciate it. Noting that silence, the editorialist explained, women had taken the initiative and staged a public demonstration—they held a parade. What better way to draw attention to their existence and success, and to distinguish themselves among the many organizations, than to stage a parade—to march in public, in elegant dress uniform and insignia? It was a classic response and challenge, an act in the political arena of social respectability. Women were resisting being made invisible by the very organization whose societal respectability their groups had worked so hard to achieve.

This was in 1828, after the General Conference placed women's collective efforts under the rubric "Daughters of Conference." The editorial confirmed that there were an assortment of successful groups who also sought recognition of women's work. Politically, women were not content to establish associations, muster their collective energies in support of the Church, and donate their labors for the betterment of the whole without receiving specific recognition for it, particularly as there were no denominational positions for them. The amorphous category of "women's work" made no distinction between the Daughters of Conference and the variety of other gender-specific associations that functioned within African Methodism. A brief acknowledgment of the older organization was insufficient reflection of the diversity of women's activities and groups that existed at the time.

The financial effectiveness of women's organizations was cause enough for them to presume that they deserved more public and differentiated recognition. Monetary contributions from Daughters of Conference groups were replicated throughout the denomination, as women made donations specifically to support the clergy. In 1855, Daughters of Conference groups in the Philadelphia Annual Conference contributed $102 from a fund-raising tea; in that same year the New York Daughters of Conference surpassed Philadelphia with a contribution of $202.68 to the clergy in its district. In 1864, when women's earlier demands for recognition were producing results, Daughters organizations in New York were so effective that they received public recognition in the denominational newspaper, the *Christian Recorder*: "The Daughters of Conference in the New York District are becoming famous."[4] In the antebellum period, similar organizations outside New York and Philadelphia were equally active, though not as visible. For example, the Daughters of the New England Annual Conference were consistent contributors to the economic stability of their pastors.

As another example, not specifically from a Daughters of Conference group, was the board of trustees at Metropolitan Church in Washington, D.C., which affirmed that women's societies were indispensable to the congregation's well-being. The churchwomen there had donated "extra improvements by way of Lamps, Alter [*sic*] Seating of the Gallery." In a local church of New Orleans, the debt on the building was liquidated because of "the sisters," and a women's aid society was equally important to eliminating the mortgage on a local church's building in Cincinnati.[5] Clearly, women's organizations were an established and essential component of denominational life, as well as an important source of funds for local churches. The success of their gender-specific organizations is directly relevant to our consideration of women, power, and the Church.

It is apparent that although there were no positions for women when African Methodism was formed, and though no Methodist body included women in its hierarchy, as early as 1828 the numerical presence of AME women outstripped the ability of the denomination to integrate their activities without structural changes. To introduce women into formal arrangements violated cultural norms of Protestantism and American society; therefore it would tend to undermine the African American struggle for social respectability. However, not to open organizational space for women only increased the number and intensity of protests like the 1828 parade. The contradictions implicit in the situation did not disappear, and they foretold future tensions.

The early proliferation and success of women's organizations also meant that the AME Church would have parallel structures. One was for women, who functioned effectively in various roles but held no positions of authority. Another structure was for men, who occupied positions of formal authority but depended on the numbers, organizations, and resources of women. The pattern was significant and cannot be ignored if the changes women caused in their denomination are to be assessed accurately. The parallel structures began to grow when women organized the first useful, gender-specific group in 1816; thereafter the model was replicated as the denomination added new local congregations. The Church's legislative body acknowledged an interdependent relationship with women's groups when it publicly accepted Daughters of Conference 1827 contributions, and it formally established the tie in 1828. The relationship was interdependent in that women's membership, organization, and resources were indispensable to the survival and success of the young church, and without the success of the AME Church its women members had fewer social spaces for self and collective expression.

This pattern of social relationships within the Church was further concretized as women established additional mutual-aid organizations, and as the Church, particularly the community based clergy, became dependent on the material success of these groups for its own functioning. Women were accumulating sources of power.

In itself, the existence of parallel and interdependent structures did not guarantee that churchwomen would participate in decision making or mean that they possessed all the sources of power necessary to implement their will and make structural changes.

But the network of organizations was an important channel through which the women's struggle for change could unfold. Through the network they learned the rights, responsibilities, and behaviors associated with organizational survival, not to mention *Robert's Rules of Order*, which guided all meetings. In the formula that produces power, organization is more important than numerical strength; it can often outstrip resources, and women were organized.[6]

The women's network was also a space for social discourse, where they regularly gathered and explored ideas of common concern. When collective discussion had clarified and affirmed the importance of various issues, they could be presented in public arenas as collective concerns of African American women. In this regard, once again, the experiences of AME women are consistent with those of Baptist women studied by Evelyn Higginbotham, wherein, as she has revealed, patterns of public discourse among African American women regularly formed within Church circles.[7]

ORGANIZATIONAL FUNCTIONING

The organizations that AME women formed were, then, important arenas of socialization and education, but in them women also learned about the day-to-day operations of their denomination. Though they were not authorized to hold most Church offices, women's service in certain positions throughout the nineteenth century undergirded their efforts to carve out an organizational space in the denomination.

Women actively performed duties associated with most positions in the laity, as well as in the lower levels of the ministerial hierarchy. In these roles they began to understand the Church's infrastructure with regard to decision making and the exercise of power. They served as teachers, exhorters, evangelists, class leaders, and preachers, although they performed in these positions without official assignment or authority.

The position of teacher was one in which the presence of women was particularly strong and visible. The minutes of the 1859 Baltimore Annual Conference, for example, noted that there were eighty-two women among the 158 teachers in eleven local churches. In East

Florida, Mary E. Miller, Sister Mary Still, Josephine Jones-Still, Susan L. Waterman, G. G. Waterman, Martha D. Sickles-Greenwood, and M. S. Comer were all founders and teachers of schools within AME congregations.[8] The *Christian Recorder* reported that Mrs. Emily Rodney and Mrs. Amelia Howard "labored in Virginia" with the Freedmen's Bureau from the end of the Civil War through the 1880s.

Women teachers were particularly engaged in the South during the Reconstruction era; Jane M. Lynch was such a teacher. She was a free-born African American woman who had been educated in the Northeast. In May 1863, after hearing the farewell sermon of a minister who became one of the first AME missionaries in the South since the 1822 Denmark Vessey rebellion, Jane Lynch moved from the comfort of her urban surroundings to the turmoil of the wartime South. She was one of the first African American women to volunteer to teach among the recently freed slaves near Beaufort, South Carolina. The AME Church in that area was not yet sufficiently organized to have a Sunday school, but when she was transferred to Elkton, Maryland, Jane Lynch filled the position of teacher in the congregation of that community. There she also wrote brief articles about her activities for the denominational newspaper.[9]

The ability of women to become teachers with relative ease and without opposition was a product of several sociological factors, factors that affected all of the African American community. Under the prevailing mid-nineteenth-century American attitude toward gender roles and social boundaries, the socialization and education of young children was considered appropriate work for women. As the Civil War came to a close and a need arose to instruct the thousands of emancipated African Americans, social attitudes expanded to include women as appropriate professional teachers as well. These expanding norms of gender roles provided the social flexibility to allow AME women to instruct adults as well as children, without threat to or challenge from the male leadership or Church hierarchy. Equally important was the fact that literate men who might have become teachers were systematically guided into the ministry. The Church desperately needed pastors, to minister to and lead a rapidly increasing membership. Any man who could read and write was automatically pointed in the direction of ordination, to take on the responsibilities of a congregation and clergy. Women were prohibited from the ordained clergy, but social attitudes generally supported them in the nurturing duties related to teaching, even of adults.

As teachers, women acquired critical knowledge about their faith tradition, Methodism; about the biblical texts upon which that tradition was built; and about denominational rules, policies, and customs. In addition they learned about pedagogical techniques, the dynamics of group interaction, organizational record keeping, and other duties and responsibilities related to the practice of African Methodism. Over the century, each new generation of women built on this knowledge and used it to further the cause of women's inclusion into AME structure.

Women served with equal success as exhorters and evangelists— divinely inspired persons who spoke passionately of their faith as encouragement to others to convert, join, or strengthen their Christian practice—and women contributed significantly to the Church's expansion in these roles. For example, Harriet Felson Taylor was the second woman member of the Washington, D.C., assembly that was the first congregation to unite with African Methodism after its 1816 founding. This congregation was an important symbol of AME stability in the early mid-Atlantic regional growth. Harriet "distinguished herself as the First Female Exhorter" at the Union Church. Rebecca Jackson, who resided in Philadelphia during the formative era of the Church, recorded in her diary that AME women regularly functioned as exhorters. She felt strongly that gospel work did not need human authorization, and when the Church refused to give official license to women as exhorters or allow them to be ordained into the ministry, Mrs. Jackson resigned her AME membership.[10] It was a radical step for an African American woman of the 1830s, given that no Christian body of the time ordained women; most AME women took less extreme action. Some continued to serve as exhorters and evangelists in local, particularly rural, congregations.

In New Jersey, Deliah Johnson not only functioned as an evangelist but was instrumental in establishing the 1830s congregations of Mount Holly and Mount Laurel (later called Evesham). Deliah was exemplary in evangelistical duties, "to save souls and build up churches and congregations," though she had no authority from the denomination.[11] Later in the century, in Minneapolis, Minnesota, Mrs. Lena Doolin Mason would always be remembered for "her five months' work in churches" of that city. She was an evangelist who was instrumental in converting at least 1,617 souls. In the South Carolina Annual Conference, from 1873 through the end of the century, Charlotte S. Riley, Mary C. Palmer, Melinda M. Cotton, Emma V. Johnson, and Mary L. Harris were evangelists who gave extensive reports to the Philadelphia Annual Conference.[12] Throughout the century, women's presence in positions of exhorter and evangelist provided their gender with needed knowledge about denominational operations. At the same time, their numerical representation in that unauthorized service was a reminder to the AME Church that it had no official place for women to serve. The women were a challenge.

Class leader was another role in which women functioned without official approval. Class leaders were responsible for qualitatively strengthening the participation of a local congregation. Men were authorized to serve in that position, wherein they guided small groups of members in their duties as African Methodists. Class leaders were appointed by pastors and charged with overseeing the spiritual and social lives of twelve or more members assigned to their classes. Leaders were to be familiar with the current state of each member's knowledge about African Methodist doctrine and polity, and with each person's physical well-being; they were to keep the congregation's pastor and Official Board informed of these matters. On a weekly basis, class leaders were to collect financial donations from members and, during meetings of the Official Board, deliver the funds to a steward. It was preferred that class leader positions, like those of exhorter and evangelist, be filled by men who were licensed ministers or ordained clergymen.

A few women served as class leaders. In Bordentown, New Jersey, for example, "the class was led for some time by a Christian female." At Union Bethel Church in Washington, D.C., in similar fashion, Lethee Bell Tanner served as a class leader for several years. She had been "the first woman who had her name enrolled on the Roll of Members" of that congregation.[13] Later in the century, Sarah Gorham also served as a class leader. She had been born on December 25, 1832, in Frederick, Maryland, and by 1885 was a member of Charles Street Church in Boston,

Massachusetts. It is significant that Sarah Gorham was a woman of no ordinary character. She had acquired an international reputation as an effective evangelist and undoubtedly was allowed to serve as class leader in Boston because of it. Equally of note is that Sarah led a small class, in a large and well established urban congregation, where the success of her work would be unlikely to overshadow that of men in similar roles.

The position of class leader was in the laity, not the clerical hierarchy, but neither congregations nor the denomination could operate if class leader positions went vacant for long periods of time. Despite their importance in congregational life, however, class leaders had no authority to speak for the denomination or its spiritual beliefs.

A significance of women functioning as class leaders, as of their service as teachers, exhorters, and evangelists, was that in that way throughout the century they acquired vital knowledge about the inner workings of African Methodism. What they learned about customs, norms, and procedures associated with keeping a local congregation viable was important for strengthening their gender organizations. Equally important was how this detailed knowledge gave women the ability and practical opportunity to refine their skills of community organizing, which also improved their organizations. It was an important knowledge when the time came to capitalize on accumulated sources of power to bring about change in favor of women in the national Church structure. As the century unfolded, the quality of women's functioning and the effectiveness of their organizations improved, and women became more familiar with how to organize as a prerequisite of power.

Again, there was little opposition to women serving in any of the positions of the laity, and little or no protest to the fact that they were violating the cultural expectation that men would occupy official Church roles. No one seemed moved to contest the fact that women were functioning without the sanction of denominational law, because their contributions to Church expansion were twice as important as their unofficial service. The highest priority was to develop a strong African Methodist presence, and there were not enough dependable men to fill every position in the clergy and the laity.

As the century reached its midpoint, however, the numerical strength of women and their consequent power increased. Their work in support of the Church became conspicuously effective. The exclusively male AME hierarchy began to feel threatened, and moved to reiterate organizational boundaries of women's services. However, there had been opposition to women preachers even in the early stages of the denomination's development, before gender boundaries were tightened.

Local and traveling preachers, ordinarily men, were assigned and authorized by bishops to expound the Christian gospel. Local preachers were firmly, if not exclusively, associated with specific communities; traveling preachers moved between geographic areas. When invited by congregational leaders they delivered sermons at worship, revival, camp meeting, or other services. The gender and moral practices of the Victorian era dictated that men should lead in the public aspects of congregations and church. Accordingly, the AME Church ordained only men into the clergy, assigning them as local or traveling preachers. The major criterion for fulfilling this role was the individual's divine calling to preach.

Despite social norms and denominational policy of an all-male clergy, many African Methodist women felt God had called them to the gospel ministry, and they refused to allow human prohibitions to deter them from responding to those divine instructions. These women obeyed the spiritual calling and acted as traveling preachers. As traveling preachers women were less likely to threaten the male clergy. In this way also, local congregations had the freedom to evaluate by their own criteria the authenticity of a woman's calling as well as her hermeneutic skills. This also strengthened the social stability that the AME Church, as a religious organization, could offer the African American community. That is to say, the community was not impeded in the strengthening of its infrastructure during the first half of the nineteenth century by an internal fight over who could and should preach the gospel.

Nevertheless, preaching women, even as traveling preachers, represented the undeniable fact that women were struggling for a place in Church polity. Jarena Lee was the earliest African American woman preacher on record. In 1849 she published her autobiography, in which she reports that she traveled with "other AME ministers in the New York and New Jersey areas" between 1820 and 1830. Her record of her activities can be corroborated and validated as historical fact.[13] Mrs. Zilpha Elaw of Maryland has already been

cited as a traveling preacher who refused to be intimidated by tightened restrictions after the 1822 Denmark Vessey rebellion. Harriet
Felson Taylor also traveled and preached in the Washington, D.C.,
area. Along with her other duties, she was described as a preacher
associated with Union Bethel Church. Rachel Evans, a member of a
New Jersey Annual Conference congregation, was similarly mentioned as an AME "preacheress of no ordinary ability." Mrs.
Evans's reputation went even farther: "she could rouse a congregation at any time and was better than her husband."[15]

Minutes of denominational conferences as early as 1848 chron-
icle how preaching women aroused both attention and opposition. Authorities complained that these women believed themselves divinely commissioned to preach. There was even a general
understanding that the women had organized themselves into an
operational network and issued themselves preaching assignments
in local churches. Whether or not such a network existed, by
1850, a leading bishop, Daniel Payne, felt compelled to respond
to the threat of such an organization, real or imagined. However,
he considered the women to be a minor annoyance, with no potential for the future; such women, he said, were "a rope of
sand."[16] But even so, the bishop's public and published comments
attest to the fact that even in the antebellum period, African
Methodist women were demonstrating sophisticated knowledge
about religious organization. Later we will see how women used
these acquired skills, as well as their organizations, to gain access
to denominational decision making.

The 1865 victory of the North brought both an end to the Civil
War and a flood of new members into the AME Church. The majority of these once-enslaved new members were women, just as in
communities of free blacks when the Church had expanded into
the territories. With the close of the Civil War, therefore, the AME
hierarchy was again confronted with the question of how to contain, within existing organizational arrangements, women's
Church participation—a participation that had become indispensable. Although the focus of this book here is on women's accumulation of power to challenge the Church structure, it is worth
a small detour to summarize briefly the postwar context that produced the surge in new membership, with the corollary increase in
women's organizations.

African Methodist ministers who accompanied federal military forces during the Civil War had brought southern blacks a message both of Christianity and of the possibility of membership in an independent African American organization. For the emancipated women and men of the South, this was an opportunity to affirm their commitment to collective racial identity within the new circumstances of freedom in a United States that they and their ancestors had helped build. It was also a chance to be part of organized Christian tradition and to take an active part in the advancement of people of African descent in the United States. These freed men and women no longer needed to be subject to the organizational supervision and authority of European Americans. It was an opportunity to be a free people and to demonstrate a capacity for collective self-determination.

Entire congregations of recently emancipated women and men joined the AME Church through the ministers who had accompanied the victorious Northern armies. Buildings and properties used by the ex-slaves and abandoned by fleeing southern European Americans were turned over by the occupying forces to the black denomination.[17] This new method of Church expansion accounted for a rapid and precipitous increase in membership, buildings, and other real estate. Women were in the majority of the new Church members, just as they had accounted for the majority of the general African American population of the thirteen states of the Confederacy. This remarkable influx of southern congregations, from a general black population where women were the majority and thus the majority congregants, propelled the AME Church to new social prominence. However, with so many new female members, the question of women's participation understandably became a point of organizational tension.

Even before the Civil War, the Church leadership had discussed the participation of women in denominational structure, particularly preaching women. At each General Conference from 1848 through 1860, delegates had discussed women's presence and unauthorized functioning in the Church polity. The discussions centered on preaching women, but the men were definitely concerned with women's overall numerical presence as well as with the effectiveness of their activities in support of the denomination. Men repeatedly discussed the pressing issue of whether or not to bring women into the formal structure. A few delegates voiced support of the idea, but there were never enough votes for the topic to be seriously considered or approved. However, even as men persisted in prohibiting women from official preaching positions and in denying them ordination, they had to deal with women's numerical presence and "unauthorized" successes, without having a negative effect on Church growth.

The men could continue to deny women official position in the structure and thereby risk losing members and the benefits of women's work, or they could establish a position for women and abandon an exclusively male Church polity. Both alternatives seemed unacceptable; the hierarchy therefore found a third alternative—"stewardess" position—and effectively skirted the issue yet again. In 1868, when because of the accessions from the southern states the hierarchy could no longer overlook the increasing number of churchwomen, the General Conference voted to create the position of "stewardess" in the laity. This action gave the appearance of gender inclusion, but, like the 1828 designation of the Daughters of Conference, the new position was created after women had already established themselves as effective participants in a variety of denominational roles without official approval. Again, the Church hierarchy was taking advantage of the product of women's work without incorporating women into the polity.

A stewardess was a designated female assistant to men who were "stewards" in local congregations. Women could be appointed stewardesses by the vote of a congregation's stewards, and at the discretion of its pastor. A congregation was required to have no less than three and no more than nine stewardesses. But none of this gave women denominational authority because their new position had "no legislative or judicial discretion." A stewardess was responsible for the care of female members of a congregation and was accountable to its stewards, class leaders, and local ministers—all positions reserved to men.[18]

Historical records show that women did not gravitate to the new position until later in the twentieth century. At the denomination's centennial celebration, only twenty-eight women were identified as stewardesses among a Church population of over forty thousand members.[19] Instead, as the nineteenth century moved to a close, women functioned as preachers, evangelists, and in most other positions of the laity, as well as stewardesses. Their expectations of a gender-inclusive Church had not yet been fully met, but the visionary goal had become clearer. It would be more difficult to contain women.

MISSIONARY ORGANIZATION

The strongest and most overt expression of organization by women as a source of power occurred after the Civil War and after the creation of the stewardess position—that is, after 1868. It was in the administrative arena of missionary work. Missionary activities had been part of the denominational agenda for some time, but previous efforts had been led by churchmen, and by February 1874 they were deteriorating. Without making an explicit plea for help but aware of the fund-raising success of the Daughters of Conference and of other women's organizations, the men turned to women to redeem the missionary work. They suggested that women "ought to organize a Women's Missionary Society," and they voted to authorize such an organization. On May 8, 1874, the male leadership issued a call to the wives of several bishops to form such a society. The women gathered in Washington, D.C., to organize a "missionary society . . . for the evangelization of the world, especially of the island of Haiti, and to secure the cooperation of the sisters."[20] A convention of all AME women was held in August, and the Women's Parent Mite Missionary (WPMM) Society was created.

The Missionary Society became yet another organizational space in which women enhanced and extended their knowledge and experience in the functioning of the denomination. A second Missionary Society, formed in 1896, guaranteed southern women an organizational domain under their own leadership. These formal arrangements were extensions of individual women's missionary efforts that had functioned before the women's societies were formed. Women now added missionary societies to their other parcels of organization—critical necessities for changing Church structure.

NOTES

1. Evelyn Higginbotham, *Righteous Discontent: The Women's Movement in the Black Baptist Church, 1880-1920* (Cambridge, Mass.: Harvard University Press, 1993); Cheryl Townsend Gilkes, personal interview, Boston, Massachusetts, 1985, and at Annual Meeting of Society for the Scientific Study of Religion, Montreal, Canada, 1998.

2. Daniel Payne, *The Semi-Centenary and the Retrospection of the African Methodist Episcopal Church in the United States* (Baltimore: Sherwood, 1866), 27–32.

3. Editorial, *Freedom's Journal*, August 15, 1828, 166.

4. *Christian Recorder*, June 18, 1864.

5. See Benjamin W. Arnett, *Proceedings of the Semi-Centenary Celebration of the African Methodist Episcopal Church of Cincinnati* (Cincinnati: H. Watkin, 1874), 121.

6. See Henry M. Robert, III, William J. Evans, Daniel H. Honemann, and Thomas J. Balch, *Robert's Rules of Order*, rev. 10th ed. (Cambridge: Perseus, 1970).

7. Higginbotham, *Righteous Discontent*.

8. AME Church, *Minutes of the Baltimore Annual Conference of the African Methodist Episcopal Church* (Baltimore: James Young, 1859).

9. See *The Christian Recorder*, February 24, April 21, and July 7, 1866.

10. Jarena Lee, *The Religious Experience and Journal of Mrs. Jarena Lee: Giving an Account of Her Call to Preach the Gospel* (Philadelphia: n.p., 1849:15); Charles Wesley, *Richard Allen, Apostle of Freedom* (Washington, D.C.: Associated, 1937), 195–98; John F. Cook, "Extract of Proceedings Annual Conference of the African Methodist Episcopal Church for the Baltimore District, Washington City, April 28, 1840," manuscript, Cook Family Papers, box 1, Washington, D.C., Moorland-Spingarn Research Center, Howard University, c. 1840, 2; Rebecca Jackson, *Gifts of Power: The Writings of Rebecca Jackson, Black Visionary, Shaker Eldress*, ed. Jean McMahon Humez (Amherst: University of Massachusetts Press, 1981); Amanda Berry Smith, *Amanda Smith: The Colored Evangelist* (Chicago: Christian Witness, 1921).

11. Joseph S. Thompson, *Bethel Gleanings* (Philadelphia: Robert J. Holland, 1881); Joseph Morgan, *Morgan's History of the New Jersey Conference of the African Methodist Episcopal Church from 1872–1887* (Camden, N.J.: S. Chew, 1887), 70–82.

12. See Daniel W. Culp, *Twentieth Century Negro Literature* (New York: Arno, 1969), 38, 444; *African Methodist Episcopal Journal of Proceedings of the Twenty-fifth Session of the New Jersey Annual Conference* (Philadelphia: AME Publishing House, c. 1897); *African*

Methodist Episcopal Journal of Proceedings of the Eighty-second Session of the Philadelphia Annual Conference of the African Methodist Episcopal Church (Philadelphia: AME Publishing House, 1898), 91–99; and African Methodist Episcopal Church, *Journal of Proceedings of the Eighty-first Session of the Philadelphia Annual Conference of the African Methodist Episcopal Church* (n.p., 1897), 4.

13. Morgan, *New Jersey Conference*, 67; Cook, "Extract," 2; Alexander Walker Wayman, *Cyclopaedia of African Methodism* (Baltimore: Methodist Episcopal Book Depository, 1882), 57.

14. Compare Lee, *Journal*, 34; and Daniel A. Payne, *History of the African Methodist Episcopal Church* (Nashville, Tenn.: African Methodist Sunday School Union, 1891), 41.

15. James A. Handy, *Scraps of African Methodist Episcopal History* (Philadelphia: AME Book Concern, n.d.), 345; Cook, "Extract," 2; Wayman, *Cyclopaedia*; Morgan, *New Jersey Conference*.

16. Payne, *History*, 237.

17. For discussions of the number of blacks that joined the AME Church and left white denominations, see Payne, *History*, 471–72; Harry V. Richardson, *Dark Salvation: The Story of Methodism as It Developed among Blacks in America* (New York: Anchor, 1976), 195; and William Pope Harrison, *The Gospel among the Slaves: A Short Account of Missionary Operations among the African Slaves of the Southern States* (Nashville, Tenn.: Methodist Episcopal Church South, 1893), 318–24.

18. Henry McNeal Turner, *The Genus and Theory of Methodist Polity or the Machinery of Methodism* (Philadelphia: Publication Department of the AME Church, 1885), 166.

19. This figure is my count of the stewardesses listed in Richard R. Wright Jr., *Centennial Encyclopaedia of the African Methodist Episcopal Church* (Philadelphia: AME Book Concern, 1916), 169, 187, 208, 243, 282, 369.

20. Wright, *Centennial Encyclopaedia*, 324–25.

4

✟

Indispensable Resources

Power, whatever its basis, in a social relationship allows people or groups to carry out their will even when there is resistance. The foremothers of the twentieth- and twenty-first-century African Methodist women handed down an opportunity to stand for, and be elected to, the highest position in the Church hierarchy, that of bishop. AME women of the nineteenth century struggled hard and transferred to women of the twentieth and twenty-first centuries sources of power that were to so change the denomination that a woman, the Rev. Vashti Murphy McKenzie, was ultimately elected to the episcopacy.

Throughout the second half of the nineteenth century, women consolidated their numerical strength into gender-specific organizations and in them another source of power. Working within the network of their organizations, women simultaneously amassed the third source of power, resources—resources important to the exercise of power in the Church, an exercise that eventually produced structural changes. Contemporary churchwomen have inherited and built upon historical familiarity, experienced knowledge, and the skills of using the power of numbers, organization, and resources to achieve women's goals.

Resources, as a source of power, can be material or nonmaterial, as long as members of the larger social relationship value them. Women's ability to accumulate both types of resources valued by AME Church members was directly linked to, if not dependent on, their gender-specific organizations. The groups were formed to strengthen the new denomination and thereby improve social conditions of the African American community at large. The pattern of black women forming mutual-aid organizations for the betterment of community emerged from their collective cultural memory. It was a memory of enslaved women who had gathered the resources of a few to sustain individual lives of the many. It was also a memory implanted from their African heritage. The work of Stanley Mintz and Richard Price, as well as of Rosalyn Terborg-Penn, Filomina Steady, and others, confirms this fact.

African Americans in the Western Hemisphere created patterns of social organization based on existing conditions but within a consciousness derived from their African heritage.[1] In their ancestral societies, women's social participation had been regularly manifested in gender-specific groups, and African Methodist women in the United States, despite and because of social conditions that confronted them, would organize similar gender-specific groups. They accumulated a variety of resources through their organizations and used both means to help sustain the Church and the larger African American community. The pattern was typical for African American women; it characterized their distinct feminist behavior.[2] In the context of this exploration of the historical dynamics of women, power, and the Church, we turn to resources.

MATERIAL RESOURCES

Real estate and furnishing constituted the first category of material resources that women possessed and made available to the denomination. These donations were vital as they helped stabilize growth at a time when the Church's survival was not assured. For example, at the Church's beginnings in Philadelphia in 1787, the Free African Society met in a woman's house with her furnishings. These earliest efforts at organizing an independent black religious association were strengthened by the fact that Sarah Dougherty possessed a house and allowed it to be used for society meetings.

Several circumstances described in the previous chapter on organization suggested that real estate, furnishings, and other similar materials were indeed resources. There we saw that in 1841 the congregation in Washington, D.C., praised women for "extra improvements by way of Lamps, Alter [*sic*] Seating of the Gallery." In 1876, when Quinn Chapel of Flint, Michigan, was organized, Lucretia Wright was a charter member of the congregation and donated the property on which the church parsonage was built. Priscilla Baltimore, of St. Louis, like hundreds of other nineteenth-century women, made her house available as a meeting place for an African Methodist congregation. Women possessed and contributed real estate as well as physical space where organization could occur; they even saw that the spaces were furnished. These contributions were but one important contribution of women in the category of material resources.[3]

Labor

Labor is another highly significant material resource, albeit one that is often overlooked in connection with women's assets. As the numerical majority of the Church's membership, women were also its primary labor force. Because their share of the membership never fell below 51 percent during the century, they were an abundant and active pool of labor for the Church. In the construction of a local church in New Orleans, for example, the congregation apparently decided not to use its limited reserve of skilled men for carrying bricks and mortar; they were needed for the skilled work of carpentry and masonry. Nevertheless, bricks and mortar had to be transported to locations where the craftsmen were working. The women of the Church carried them.[4]

In Philadelphia, in 1844, a mob of European Americans threatened to ransack, if not burn, a local AME Church. The black congregants were unsure how to repel the crowd. They had worked exceptionally hard to acquire this sanctuary and were not about to see it destroyed by this capricious act of racism, but what could be done? The women initiated the defensive fight by deploying members to various strategic locations, particularly second floor windows and openings. When the mob was within striking distance, the cry went out, and the AME women and men threw stones, clubs, and pepper at the approaching whites. The Methodists won the day.[5]

Even the denomination's founding benefited from women's labor. The women who attended the 1816 organizing meeting in Philadelphia provided the attending clergymen with mended clothing and with food that sustained them in the meeting. The women offered their labor in cooking and serving. These are only a few examples of the value of women's labor as a resource of the AME Church; further historical research should easily expose a plethora of others. Women converted their numerical strength in the Church into the critical resource of labor.

Finances

Daughters of Conference organizations were the social domains from which AME women began to acquire funds as a resource, and to use them to benefit the denomination. Through collective effort women organized public sales of cakes, pies, fruit preserves, and other foodstuffs to earn small—and not so small—incomes. This fund-raising method was not uncommon in African American communities and AME women used it effectively.[6] Funds earned were contributed to the Church.

A first and important financial contribution from such collective work was the 1827 donation from the Daughters of Conference to help support the Church's clergymen. In Philadelphia, the Daughters of the Annual Conference contributed $102 in 1855; in the same year, at the New York Annual Conference, the Daughters of Conference gave $202.68. The New England conference was not as populous as many others, making fund-raising a more difficult task, but between 1852 and 1862, Daughters of Conference in congregations of that region gave $205.16 to conference ministers. After the Civil War, between 1866 and 1872, they contributed another $470.[7]

In 1854, women's accumulation of resources in the social equation that equaled power was extended to real estate. In the New Orleans congregation, which was attempting to pay off the mortgage on its church building, women's gender-specific societies began a variety of fund-raising activities. The efforts were highly successful, and the congregation's historical records read, "Sisters . . . realized about two thousand dollars in cash."[8] This was an extraordinary sum for the antebellum period. At Metropolitan Church in Washington, D.C., churchwomen raised a hundred dollars of the total $489.97 raised, while at Allen Temple in Cincinnati, Ohio, a women's aid society contributed more than two thousand dollars toward the debt on their church building.[9]

The financial contributions of women were an indispensable part of denominational administration within the conference structure. The annual gatherings of congregational delegates rarely proceeded without the women's donations, and each ministerial delegate expected to receive a portion of such funds. The agenda for these meetings consistently allocated time for formally receiving the women's contributions. If the item was found to have been omitted, the error was of such significance that time was immediately reappropriated for the women.

The sheer numerical superiority of women, inside and outside of the denomination, was a contributing factor in their ability to garner financial resources and donate them to the Church. There were more women than men to do fund-raising, as well as larger numbers from whom to solicit funds. But this link between numbers and resources must not be overemphasized. The discretionary income of women, available for donations, was less than proportionate to that of men in the Church. Their salaries from productive work, when they earned any, were always less than the salaries of men. Nevertheless, the important fact is that prior to the Civil War women were effective at fund-raising and they repeatedly donated money to their church.

During and after the war, the denomination operated a "Two Cents Plan," whereby each member of a congregation was assessed an extra two cents per year to be donated to the general fund and used for maintaining the connectional body. Unlike local bodies, the leadership of the denomination as a whole had no direct link to its constituencies. Consequently, additional money raised by the women's network was regularly allocated to the general fund. With the membership increases associated with the Civil War, came parallel increases in fiscal needs at the denominational level. The 1872 General Conference, adjusting to the new situation, upgraded the Two Cents Plan into a "Dollar Money System." It required pastors to collect one dollar extra each year from, or for, each registered member of their congregations and forward the money to the denomination. A finance department, which replaced the general fund, managed Dollar Money. Both of these new creations were aimed at improving the scope and quality of publications, educational facilities, itinerant ministries, and general administrative work of the denomination's Annual Conferences.[10]

Table 4.1   Money Given to the General Fund of the Finance Department: Quadrennial Periods, 1872–1900

Period Received	Dollars
1872–1876	$ 95,554.11
1876–1880	99,925.68
1880–1888*	368,895.86
1888–1892	313,341.44
1892–1896	351,942.09
1896–1900	406,074.26
Total	**$1,635,733.44**

Source: Wright (1947), 377.
*This amount was received over eight years, not four.

Historical records do not always make gender distinctions among Dollar Money contributors, but on the basis of a count (within a 10 percent sample of total donors) of those whose first names are normally associated with females, women appear to represent the majority between 1888 and 1892. In the 1885 list of Dollar Money contributors from California, for example, of the 179 donor names, eighty-two were probably women's. The Illinois list of that same year had 521 contributors of Dollar Money, of whom 264 names were identifiably those of women. This pattern held true even when the total money contributed by women was not the largest amount given.[11] Table 4.1 lists total receipts to the finance department between 1872 and 1900.

By 1900, the general fund had received more than a quarter of a million dollars for its last three quadrennial periods. Between 1872 and 1900 this independent organization of African Methodists—who had been enslaved until 1863, who were first generation free black citizens and descendants of free African Americans—accumulated and managed more than one and a half million dollars. The AME Church was an establishment of undeniable financial strength at the close of the nineteenth century, and women's contributions had been irreplaceable in making that strength possible.

Sunday school donations were another arena in which the feminist survival network of churchwomen could accumulate financial leverage as a source of organizational power. For many nineteenth-century African Americans, church-based schools were the only contact with formal education, and much of AME women's service and church participation occurred through local Sunday school programs. Local students as well as teachers regularly gave money in Sunday school activities. In 1834 the denomination organized a Sunday School Union. Seven years later, the Annual Conference of Baltimore reported nine schools, 482 students, and thirty-seven teachers—and this was but one conference. Theoretically, since Sunday schools existed throughout the connectional Church, the national body should have received from them more than sufficient funds to supply local congregations with educational and teaching literature, as well as other materials. The financial donations would presumably have been enough to fulfill other economic obligations as well.

However, Sunday school was not an area in which women concentrated on the gathering of funds as a material resource. For unknown reasons, women did not put their monetary resources into the program and did not use this avenue to accumulate power. As late as 1883, the Sunday School Union's annual income was only $1,839. In other arenas, when women decided to do fund-raising, they could collect that amount in a single offering. Women were Sunday school teachers and students, certainly, but they did not donate significant amounts of money to that program.

In general however, women's material contributions to the AME Church were irreplaceable for denominational development and their responsibility for these contributions accrued power to women. They were not permitted into the clergy, and their activities in Church organizational positions were not authorized and were rarely honored or credited. Despite this lack of acknowledgment, however, women's contributions to their church could not be completely denied, particularly their material offerings. Also, the esteem they earned by those material contributions gave women a third source of organizational power—power that they would combine with their numbers and organization to oblige the Church to allow them officially in structural positions.

NONMATERIAL RESOURCES

Among the tripartite sources of power, nonmaterial resources can be as valuable as material ones. Denominational knowledge, formal education, community leadership, experience in service to the Church, and other such assets were nonmaterial resources that nineteenth-century women accumulated in their struggle for structural change.

Denominational Knowledge

Almost from the onset, African Methodist women functioning as teachers were responsible for socializing new members. The teacher position, as already noted, was within the structure of Church laity and normally was assigned to a man preparing to be, or already, ordained. Women who served as teachers, though never ordained, gained priceless knowledge about Methodist doctrine and about the policies and regulations that governed administration of the AME Church. They also received exposure to how all of these components functioned within the denomination. This was firsthand information of exceptional value because it made women independent citizens of their church, even if they could not yet vote beyond the level of their local congregations. In their gender-specific organizations, women had a basis of knowledge upon which to discuss and evaluate Church operations for themselves, without depending on men. Women did not have to wait for men to explain matters to them.

In addition to the biblical and religious instruction they gave their students, women teachers were also responsible for socializing members in the legalities that governed the Church—for instance, the complexity of Robert's Rules of Order for conducting meetings. Simultaneously, they served as role models for other AME women. Prior to 1818, the Baltimore congregation noted, for example, that Annie Dickerson "took under her care and instruction all of the new female converts and indoctrinated them in the duties they owed to their God and their church." Miss Mary Ann Prout was similarly recognized as the teacher of small children in the Baltimore day school.[12] Even at these initial stages, women as teachers were responsible for knowing and explaining the *Book of Discipline* and other regulations that governed African Methodism. Nor was it only in the early years that women functioned as teachers. The congregation in Lansing, Michigan, in the last quarter of the nineteenth century offered the African American community of that city its only educational program. Of the eleven people responsible for leadership in the program, six were women. Also, as the century entered its last decades, Mary E. Miller, Josephine Jones-Still, Susan L.

Waterman, and other women of eastern Florida organized and taught in congregational schools.[13]

Everywhere throughout the connectional Church and consistently throughout the century, women served as teachers of African Methodism. From these roles, they acquired data, knowledge, and experience on the tenets and regulations of the traditions. With the ability this gave them to interpret Church rulings, these women possessed a valuable nonmaterial resource, garnered through their service as teachers.

Formal Education

The AME Church, as well as the larger African American community, gave special respect to people with formal educations. Churchwomen numbered among these, and as a result education became a nonmaterial resource of power for them. They not only acquired formal education but were generally associated with things, places, and people related to education. As early as a generation and a half from its beginnings, the denomination began requiring that its ministers receive formal education. In 1863 Wilberforce University was established in Xenia, Ohio, as the center for the formal training of AME ministers. By 1900 there were some fifteen schools, colleges, and universities, with 6,500 students and teachers, under the authority of the Church.[14]

Women were directly involved in all arenas of these educational operations. They were students and teachers in almost every school and college the denomination operated. For example, of the thirty-five people who between 1886 and 1900 finished the curriculum at Paul Quinn College of Waco, Texas (which had been founded in 1872), twenty were women. Women were equally indispensable at Wilberforce, the flagship institution. From 1876 to 1880 alone, Wilberforce's president reported, women represented 119 of the 326 students enrolled. There also were three women on the faculty. Between 1870 and 1882, women accounted for ten of the forty-three graduates from the college department at the university. In its normal school program, in the same period, eleven of the twelve graduates were women.[15]

The difference in women's representation in the two categories is related to the gender-based curriculum of the university and to the social ethos of the era. The curriculum of Wilberforce's college department, where courses were specifically designed for ministerial preparation and were thus intended for men, was thought to be academically too difficult for women. The curriculum of the normal school program was one of basic literacy and was considered more appropriate for any work women might do as adults.

The fact that ten women nevertheless graduated from the college department during its first twenty years speaks to the refusal of African American women to be omitted from opportunities for higher education, and to their defiance of gender boundaries against acquiring that education. Even their numbers in the university's normal school program demonstrate that AME women acquired formal education and thereby garnered that nonmaterial asset. Nonmaterial resources like education were strong sources of power—and women were becoming educated.

Hallie Quinn Brown was exemplary among the women who acquired education through the denomination. She had been born in Pittsburgh, Pennsylvania, the youngest of six children. Her family moved to Chatham, Ontario, Canada, quite early in her life, but by 1868 she was sent back to the United States to take advantage of educational opportunities provided by the AME Church. Wilberforce University had recently opened and afforded an opportunity not offered in Chatham and not readily available to many African Americans, particularly women.

That she met admissions requirements and was accepted into the university reflects her determination, and the fact that she completed the curriculum of the college department attests to her remarkable abilities. She completed the classical scientific course of study, graduated in 1873 with six others, and received the bachelor of science degree. However, Hallie Quinn Brown also became a member of the community of educated AME women leaders in the African American community. Her prominence began to emerge when the president of Wilberforce called for alumni to return to the campus as teachers and aid the denomination in producing "educated colored teachers."[16] Hallie returned to Xenia, where she taught for many years, eventually serving as the dean of the Women's Department, and was certainly a role model for other women at Wilberforce and at other AME schools.

Community Leadership

Hallie Quinn Brown completed her degree at Wilberforce University after the Civil War, during the era of southern reconstruction. The legal prohibitions that had previously been in place against educating enslaved African Americans meant that after 1865, millions needed to be taught the basics of reading, writing, and fundamental mathematics, as well as to be introduced to the complexities of industrialized life—banking, voting, etc. There was therefore a great demand for teachers among the newly emancipated black population. Women from the AME Church were among the first teachers to travel from their homes to assist their southern sisters and brothers. Jane Lynch, as discussed earlier, was such a teacher, but Hallie Quinn Brown also went south. She taught children and adults, including elders, in South Carolina and Mississippi. However, unlike Emily Rodney and Amelia Howard of Virginia, or Jane Lynch in South Carolina, Hallie Brown did not at first remain among the southerners but returned north to join the faculty at Wilberforce. Ultimately, however, she became dean of the Women's Department at Allen University of Columbia, South Carolina, an AME school.

Hallie Quinn Brown was one of many leading educated AME churchwomen who became prominent nineteenth-century African American feminists. As such, these women were associated with community activities and organizations outside of their religious affiliation; the combination of their church work and their involvement in the wider society added community leadership to the nonmaterial sources of AME women's power.

Mary Church Terrell, Ida B. Wells Barnett, Laura Lemon, Lottie P. Stewart, and Mary E. Lee are a few of the educated feminist leaders of the era. Beyond the commonality of their education, they were all social activists. They held leadership responsibilities in whatever group they worked and their reputations as professional elocutionists were well known. They were internationally distinguished and they were all members of the African Methodist Episcopal Church. Each worked in such organizations as the Women's Christian Temperance Unions, Federations of Women's Clubs, the International Women's Congress, and as representatives of the Women's Missionary Societies to the African

Missionary Conference. These were not AME organizations, but like many associations in the network of churchwomen's groups, they were pace-setting organizations in the national field of social responsibility.

The visibility of AME women within these service organizations earned them the value and high esteem the African American community reserved for educated community leaders. This in turn added to denominational women's nonmaterial resources of community leadership and prominence, as well as education. Possession of these assets strengthened women's capacity to leverage their church numbers and organization.

Service Experience

While serving as teachers, women not only gained priceless knowledge about the denomination but accumulated service experience as a nonmaterial resource. Service experience was acquired as well through other church positions, even where women served unofficially. As noted, women were not authorized to occupy positions of, or serve as, exhorters or evangelists, for example, but they did and in so doing gained important public-speaking experience.

Exhorters were licensed lay helpers to congregational clergy—the pastors and the local and traveling preachers. Exhorters were recruited from persons noted for their ability in public prayer, to lead nonbelievers or those who had strayed, to Christian conversion. Exhorters were charged to attend local prayer meetings—whether in churches, private homes, or other locations—and were called upon to offer prayers of such faith-filled emotion that the intensity and speed of conversions was enhanced. Such exhortations regularly motivated attendees to frequent church services, if not become members of local congregations, often AME. Exhortations were ritualized affirmations of Christian faith. Exhorters, though instrumental in building religious solidarity and increasing congregational strength, were not authorized to speak directly to, or systematically treat, biblical texts.

Historical records verifying that women were authorized exhorters during the early years are yet to be uncovered, but women frequently functioned successfully in the position. Their ability to do so was related to Methodism's emphasis on interpersonal relationships in small groups. It was also related to the nature of those small groups of specialized activities into which congregations were divided, known as bands. These were usually gender-specific and proved effective in the socialization and community building needed to sustain congregational life. Women not only participated in AME band activities but regularly led them.

As already mentioned, Doritha Hill organized and conducted female prayer meetings at her Baltimore home when African Methodism originated in that city. These women met every two weeks, but from the outset their numbers were too large for one location; they soon divided and then subdivided. Mary Prout, also, "was a leader of a female prayer meeting" in Maryland during the period.[17] Wealthy Dorsey in Philadelphia was "a very exemplary Christian" who led a praying band in her congregation. Before, during, or at the close of band meetings, women would stand before the group and publicly express how their Christian faith had improved their lives. Such Christian witness and testimony was but a small step from exhorting, and women moved easily into the latter.

They functioned as successfully in the exhorter position as they had testifying in band meetings. An example was Elizabeth Cole, who was in Pennsylvania with Wealthy Dorsey: "She held many glorious prayer meetings, and many souls were brought to the saving knowledge" by her exhortations. Mrs. Jarena Lee was even given verbal authorization to be an exhorter—by the denomination's first bishop, Richard Allen. She was allowed to hold prayer meetings in her "hired house" and was encouraged to exhort as she found opportunity.[18] Even as the AME Church was establishing itself, therefore, women gained knowledge and experience through the position of exhorter. Later in the century this experience, as a nonmaterial resource, proved important in combining the three sources of power by which women ultimately compelled the denomination to include them in its organizational arrangements.

As there was no church authority for women to serve as exhorters (with the single known exception), neither was there formal sanction for the women who functioned as African Methodist evangelists for most of the nineteenth century. "Evangelists" were "carriers of the good news," people who went outside their congregational places of

residence for religious proselytizing. The evangelists' purpose was to
save souls from damnation and to increase the membership of congregations by "spiritual arguments and Bible doctrines, presented
forcibly, grandly, and eloquently." Mrs. Sophie Murray of Philadelphia fit this description. She was recorded as being an evangelist during the first decade of African Methodism. After she transferred her
membership from the city's second AME congregation to Bethel,
Mrs. Murray was acknowledged as the "first Evangelist" of Mother
Bethel Philadelphia.[19]

Rarely were there complaints about the fact that women functioned in either of these two denominational positions of the laity.
Indeed, who would start such protests? The European American
Christian, or even Protestant, community was rarely concerned
with how the comparatively small group of African Methodists
conducted its activities. As long as black churches did not visibly
and radically challenge the social norms of white male supremacy,
the AME Church was relatively free to establish its own practices.
Further, given the shortage of black men to all organizational positions in the Church, and women's numerical superiority among its
congregations, local bodies and the denomination tacitly accepted
women who demonstrated sufficient qualifications and effectiveness in vacant positions of the laity. It was more important for the
laity to have individuals who could help manage and expand congregations and who were strongly committed to African Methodism than it was to insist on the gender-based privileges of men.

Equally important to the absence of complaints about women's
activities was the fact that they served at the lowest levels of the
laity, not in the ministry or conferences. For example, neither exhorters nor evangelists, men included, had authority beyond local
congregations and neither required ordination. This point is important, because it meant that women could not use those positions
to bring about organizational changes that included women. However, power is a dynamic phenomenon that resides in social relations, not merely in official positions. The sources of power—numbers, organization, and resources—can be acquired and utilized to
change a structure without necessarily having the assistance of of-
ficeholders in the structure. This was exactly the course of action
AME women took as they functioned without authority as teachers, exhorters, evangelists, in addition to other roles. They were accumulating power useful for their rise in the Church hierarchy.

Other Intangibles

Nineteenth-century women also accumulated other resources of an intangible nature. Events and persons who were significant to the creation of African Methodism became legendary, receiving legitimacy from the fact of their contribution. Women's presence and active involvement at the beginning of every aspect of the denomination and in every geographic location clearly gained for them a right to a permanent place in the Church. They were associated with the revered traditions from which humans develop legends, and to be part of a legend was an imperceptible resource valued by all and possessed by AME women.

For example, who among African Methodists of Los Angeles, California, would have spoken against Biddy Mason, who had opened her home for the formation of the first congregation in that city? Her work lives in stories today. The same is true of Mrs. Gomez in San Francisco, Priscilla Baltimore of St. Louis, Jarena Lee in Ohio, Jane Lynch of the Reconstruction South, and a host of other women whose names emerge when one probes the Church's legends. The exclusion of women from organizational positions jeopardized the formal association of such women. We will see where women's legendary stature was combined with other sources of power to eliminate the structural exclusion of women.

Spiritual credibility was yet another nonmaterial resource that AME women accumulated in the nineteenth century. They acquired it by their understandings about supernatural intervention in human affairs. Belief in divine intervention and revelation was not unusual within the African American community; after all, its cultural heritage was the African continent. Within ontological perspectives, or worldviews, derived from Africa and sustained thereafter, there was a general comprehension that human existence and all historical life was part of, and infiltrated by, the sacred. In this understanding, material life is interwoven with all creation, and intervention and revelation from supernatural spheres are to be expected regularly.[20]

Early in the formation of the AME Church, Mrs. Jarena Lee exemplified the spiritual credibility earned by women. She recounted her dreams and visions at prayer meetings where she exhorted. These spiritual visitations had directed her to preaching. Members of the black community who heard Mrs. Lee accepted that divine intervention had assisted her work. They knew that no African American woman could single-handedly have overcome all the physical, social, and—not to forget—spiritual obstacles that confronted her attempts to preach.

Christian preaching was a calling socially perceived to be reserved for men, but Jarena Lee was a special African American woman. She was not deterred by the many men and women of the Christian community who opposed preaching women, or even by the disruptive and deadly snowstorm of 1847. Neither could personal poverty or a lack of denominational authority keep her from carrying out her divine calling. Mrs. Lee preached throughout the mid-Atlantic coast and the Ohio Valley during the infancy of African Methodism. She was a role model, calling upon other women to accept the seriousness of divine intervention, to act upon their calls to preach. By her tenacity and success, Jarena Lee opened the way for the Church and the larger African American community to view the spirituality of women as a valuable resource.[21]

Others followed in the footsteps of Jarena Lee and sustained women's spiritual credibility as a nonmaterial resource throughout the century. Among those who were known to have been anointed by the Holy Spirit was Mary A. Prout of Baltimore. How else could she have kept an entire congregation committed to the goal of an independent African Methodist Church when the society at large—particularly European Americans—were describing such an effort as futile? Later, the number of preaching women expanded by leaps and bounds, and they became catalysts for changes in the structure of the denomination. Reports to the conferences were replete with women's incredible accomplishments— such as those of Mrs. Amanda Berry Smith, an extraordinary, anointed AME woman who achieved international recognition and visibility.[22]

Amanda Berry Smith had been born into slavery in Maryland and hired out as a young girl to a family in Pennsylvania. She was converted to Christianity and by 1855, at the age of eighteen, had a vision of herself preaching to a crowd. She was close to death at the time, most likely from effects of the birth of her first of four babies (all of whom would die). The experience renewed Amanda's waning commitment to Christian sanctification and strengthened her ability to endure the hardships that were to come in her life. In 1870, after two marriages, four dead children, and constant poverty, Amanda Berry Smith attended a worship service at the Fleet Street AME congregation of Brooklyn, New York. Here she testified about her often overwhelming difficulties and her persistent faith in the divine call she had received. She told the gathering that God had given her a special message for the congregation at Mount Pisgah AME Church in Salem, New Jersey. Amanda preached to that church between January 25 and March 12, 1871, and was publicly credited with 156 conversions and 112 "accessions" to Mount Pisgah.[23]

Amanda Berry Smith continued her evangelism and became very well known for missionary activities in India and Africa. Everywhere it was the same—audiences and congregations recognized a special divine presence in this woman. She had a spiritual, nonmaterial strength, and the people discerned it. This resource was so powerful that when Amanda attended the 1872 AME General Conference, before traveling overseas, her reputation intimidated the male delegates. Mrs. Smith was identified as representing the "maniacal" movement of "those women preachers" seeking ordination.[24]

Other women also acquired for themselves and their gender the powerful resource of spiritual credibility. Lena Doolin-Mason, who joined the AME congregation of Hannibal, Missouri, in 1872, preached in nearly every state in the Union. Emily Calkins Stevens, a native of Freehold County, New York, was so reluctant to believe that a woman could expound the gospel that she had to receive three calls to preach before responding positively. These and many other women claimed divine assignments to preach the gospel and evangelize to all. This was a spiritual calling, one of infinite, though intangible, credibility. Within the nineteenth-century African American Christian community, it was another source of power, and AME women accumulated it.

Neither the totality of their resources nor their individual components were sufficient for women to realize their ultimate goals within the AME Church. However, when they combined resources with their membership numbers and their organization, women became able, given an opportunity, to carry out their will. At the same time, societal and organizational circumstances, as well as cultural boundaries that circumscribed their lives, dictated how AME women identify and seize such an opportunity. Power and the use of power by these black women, like their non-Methodist sisters in feminism, was of a distinct character. In the end, AME women did accumulate the three sources of power, and they did implement their will. This is evidenced by the fact that at the opening of the twentieth century there were three formal positions for women, plus two gender-specific missionary societies. During most of the nineteenth century none of these existed. This is not to eliminate other factors that contributed to structural changes in the denomination, but by focusing on women as active agents in the life of their church, we can better understand unseen dimensions of their reality, as well as added dimensions of the social phenomenon of power.

NOTES

1. See Stanley Mintz and Richard Price, *African American Culture: An Anthropological Perspective* (Boston: Beacon, 1976; repr., with preface by authors, 1992); Ruth Simms-Hamilton, "Toward a Paradigm of African Diaspora Studies," in *Creating a Paradigm and Research Agenda for Comparative Studies of the Worldwide Diaspora of African Peoples,* ed. Ruth Simms-Hamilton (Lansing: Michigan State University Press, 1988).

2. For a discussion of African and African American feminism, see Filomina Chioma Steady, "African and African American Feminism" in *Women in Africa and the African Diaspora,* ed. Rosalyn Terborg-Penn et al. (Washington, D.C.: Howard University Press, 1987), 3–24; and Darlene Clark Hine, Elsa Barkley Brown, and Rosalyn Terborg-Penn, eds., *Black Women in America: An Historical Encyclopedia* (Brooklyn, N.Y.: Calson, 1993).

3. Methodist Episcopal Church, "Board of Trustees Meeting of Union Bethel Church" The Encyclopaedia of the African Methodist Episcopal Church (Washington, D.C.: Howard University, 1941), 3; Richard R. Wright, The Encyclopaedia of the African Methodist Episcopal Church (Philadelphia: AME Book Concern, 1947), 381.

4. AME Church *Centennial Historical Souvenir of "Mother Bethel" African Methodist Episcopal Church,* (Philadelphia: Historical Society, c. 1916), 34–35.

5. John Thornton, "The History of St. James AME Church," in *A Century of African Methodism in the Deep South* (New Orleans: St. James AME Church, c. 1946), 19.

6. This method of fund-raising continues as a success in African American churches today. I have been asked by many friends and colleagues new to my community which church serves the best dinners.

7. See AME Church, *Minutes of the New England Annual Conference of the African Methodist Episcopal Church* (New Bedford, Mass.: Benjamin Lindsey, 1852), 11–13; AME Church, *Minutes of the New England Annual Conference of the African Methodist Episcopal Church in America* (New Bedford, Mass.: E. Anthony, 1859), 15; as well as AME Church, *Minutes of the New England Annual Conference of the African Methodist Episcopal Church in America* (New Bedford, Mass.: Evening Standard, 1862), 13; AME Church, *Minutes of the New England Annual Conference of the African Methodist Episcopal Church in America* (New Bedford, Mass.: E. Anthony and Sons, 1866), 12; AME Church, *Fifteenth Quadrennial Session of the General Conference of the African Methodist Episcopal Church* (unpubished, 1872), 19.

8. See AME Church, *Minutes of the Thirty-fifth Annual Conference of the New York District of the African Methodist Episcopal Church Held in Bethel Church Second Street, New York City* (New York: John W. Zuille, 1855), 19; Joseph S. Thompson, *Bethel Gleanings* (Philadelphia: Robert J. Holland, 1881), 25.

9. Alexander W. Wayman, *My Recollections of African Methodist Episcopal Minutes, or Forty Years' Experience in the African Methodist Episcopal Church* (Philadelphia: AME Book Rooms, 1882); Thornton, "History"; B. W. Arnett, *Proceedings of the Semi-Centenary Celebration of the African Methodist Episcopal Church of Cincinnati* (Cincinnati: H. Watkin, 1874), 121.

10. Benjamin Arnett, *The Budget* (unpublished, 1888), 175.

11. See AME Church, *Proceedings of the Fourteenth Annual Session of the Illinois Annual Conference of the African Methodist Episcopal Church* (Philadelphia: Christian Recorder, 1885), 22–23; and Jualynne E. Dodson, *Collective Power: Women and the AME Church* (Ph.D. diss., University of California, Berkeley, 1984).

12. Board of Trustees Minutes 1846–1847, Bethel AME Church (Baltimore: n.p., n.d.), 5.

13. Benjamin Arnett, *Proceedings of the Quarter Centennial Conference of the African Methodist Episcopal Church of South Carolina* (unpublished, 1890), 182–86.

14. Harry Richardson, *The Story of Methodism as It Developed among Blacks in America* (New York: Anchor, 1976), 107–108; U.S. Department of Commerce (1916), 495; Wright, *Encyclopaedia of the AME Church*.

15. See Jualynne E. Dodson, "To Define Black Womanhood: A Study of Black Female Graduate Students," occasional paper (Atlanta: Institute of the Black World, 1979).

16. AME Church, *Minutes of the New England Annual Conference of the African Methodist Episcopal Church* (New Bedford, Mass.: Benjamin Lindsey, 1882), 136.

17. Benjamin Tucker Tanner, *An Outline of Our History and Government for African Methodist Churchmen* (Philadelphia: n.p., 1884), 35.

18. Tanner, *An Outline*, 35; AME Church, *Centennial Historical Souvenir of "Mother" Bethel African Methodist Episcopal Church* (Philadelphia: Historical Society, 1916), 34; Jarena Lee, *The Religious Experiences and Journal of Mrs. Jarena Lee: Giving An Account of Her Call to Preach the Gospel* (Philadelphia: n.p., 1849), 15; Charles Wesley, *Richard Allen, Apostle of Freedom* (Washington, D.C.: Associated, 1935), 195–98.

19. See Henry McNeal Turner, *The Genus and Theory of Methodist Polity* (Philadelphia: Publication Department of the AME Church, 1885), 80–81; Thompson, *Bethel Gleanings*, 25.

20. John Thornton, *Africa and the Africans in the Making of the Atlantic World, 1400–1680* (New York: University of Cambridge, 1992).

21. Lee, *Religious Experiences*.

22. See AME Church, *The Doctrine and Discipline of the African Methodist Episcopal Church 19th Revised Edition* (Philadelphia: AME Book Concern, 1888).

23. *Christian Recorder* 9, no. 509, new series no. 103 (18 March 1871).

24. Amanda Berry Smith, *Amanda Smith: The Colored Evangelist* (Chicago: Christian Witness, 1921), 199–200; Adrienne Israel, *Amanda Berry Smith: From Washerwoman to Evangelist* (Lanham, Md.: Scarecrow, 1998).

5

✣

Using Power: Keeping Church

It is already clear from this story of how nineteenth-century women accumulated numbers, organization, and resources in the AME Church that women were not only coincidentally linked to these sources of power. The fact that women held no positions of church authority does not mean that they were powerless or that their growing stature was accidental. The AME Church is not the only denomination where women accumulated the sources of power and garnered an ability to implement their will. Neither is it the only independent black denomination where women used their power inside and outside church structures. Evelyn Higginbotham's research demonstrates that women possessed such ability in the National Baptist Convention; and Cheryl Townsend Gilkes's study of the Pentecostal tradition shows vividly that women participated in power relations that altered the structure of their Church. Inasmuch as these three denominations collectively account for more than half of all African American churchwomen in the United States, the experiences of African Methodists can be considered representative with respect to power in the black Church as a social institution. Therefore, we can use nineteenth-century AME experiences to see how black women used power without destroying their denominations.

Placing women and their activities in the foreground of this historical and sociological study makes clear that in the ecclesiastic arena, as in other social spheres, African American women were waging a multifaceted struggle:

- To construct a community of respectable black citizenry;
- To abolish the system of slavery and eradicate racial discrimination; and
- To contest gender discrimination in their own church.

Because women were actively engaged in all of these arenas simultaneously, one aspect or another of women's activities often overshadowed the complex, tripartite reality of their struggle, giving the impression that women had compromised or contradicted other aspects.

For example, it was mandatory—for the survival of the black community, and in turn of black women—that they be involved with an organization like the AME Church. Nothing in local or national American society guaranteed life, liberty, and the pursuit of happiness for women of African descent, particularly if they were poor, whether they were enslaved or free. Independent black congregations and denominations like the AME Church provided social space to organize the collective strengths of the community in order to struggle against slavery and racial discrimination. But at times, community cooperation against white supremacy and racism pulled African Methodist women away from their challenges to gender exclusion within the denomination.

As another example, at times women made public statements that supported the clerical patriarchy even as their actions inside the Church challenged that very structure. These contradictory realities were more a reflection of contradictions in the social status of American black women than an expression of their ideas and politics. Throughout the century, black women could not forget the social circumstances of their situation, but as churchwomen, part of their education about organizational intricacies included lessons about power and its use. A primary awareness that AME women acquired was that they indeed were in a position to seize an opportunity to implement their will; that is to say, women owned sources of power.

OWNERSHIP AND CONSCIOUSNESS

During the 1820s and 1830s, Daughters of Conference groups provided AME women with their first exposure to the perplexing and contradictory issues involved in publicly supporting independent black organizations while also challenging the gender exclusivity of those organizations. Through encounters with bishops, Daughters of Conference groups became conscious that their financial and material contributions gave women the opportunity to participate in decisions and to implement their will.

Women could have a voice in ministerial assignments to local congregations, and this was no small matter. Women in their daily lives were in constant contact with pastors, as well as the other clergymen that the bishops assigned to their churches. If a man was not compatible with the lifestyle, personalities, or general circumstances of women in a community, congregational conflict was predictable. A collaborative pastor, on the other hand, could manage the other clergy and enhance the activities of the women's groups as well as of the larger African American community. Therefore, women had a vested interest in the assignment of ministers by bishops.

Women learned that when they informed a bishop in advance of which pastors they preferred, they increased the probability that one of them would be assigned. However, they also learned that their preferences were even more likely to be honored when they reminded bishops that local women's groups were directly responsible for material resources so desperately needed and not otherwise provided by the denomination—that is, pastors' supplemental salaries, meals, clothing, housing, etc. These reminders were particularly effective when a bishop, intentionally or not, resisted women's ministerial preferences, and in response women withheld resources from the clergy of the district.

This was a negotiating basis upon which women could participate in decision making. Such space was created by the interdependent nature of power. No bishop wanted a pastor in his district to fail, but without the collaboration and cooperation of women, that could easily happen. Therefore, bishops themselves were dependent on the cooperation of women. As early as the 1820s and

1830s, and the legendary fund-raising successes of groups like the Daughters of Conference, their consistent financial and material support to clergy and local churches validated the women's reminders to the bishops. As already noted, ministers at Annual Conferences anticipated that women's contributions would supplement their livelihoods, and that if for some reason the women were not included on the agenda, the proceedings would be rearranged to accommodate them and their donations.

Eventually, informal bargaining gave way to a regularized pattern of consultation between bishops and representatives of local women's groups just prior to announcements of ministerial assignments. These advance activities allowed women to place their ministerial preferences before the bishop and to leverage the power to realize those preferences. We do not know if the women initiated the "preconference" teas, dinners, receptions, etc., but the pattern was repeated across the denomination and a departure that accommodated women was normalized.

Granted, these patterns occurred inside the Church and within the black community. They were deep structural and cultural activities, offering little or no public challenge to the authority of bishops or their right to make ministerial appointments. This sustained the perception that men in office held unilateral power. However, black women and the African American community needed strong social organizations to battle against slavery and racism. Women would not risk destroying the denomination by going public with their challenge. But neither were they prepared to abdicate their right to participate in the internal arrangements of the Church they had helped organize.

This was women's initial important lesson about using power. They were becoming aware that they possessed the sources of power and aware of what could be achieved when they combined membership, organization, and resources to assert themselves into the decision-making relationships of the Church. Interactions between women and bishops presiding at Annual Conferences had forced the Church officials to accommodate the will of women. For a while, that was sufficient.

It is important to highlight that even these early experiences of women demonstrated that authority of position was not always decisive. Similarly, AME women were not using power in terms of individual, interpersonal dominance. Women acted collectively, within the parameters of the Church's organizational structure, to persuade bishops to change the procedures.

Some might contend that AME women were doing nothing more than exercising influence, and that influence is the essence of *persuasion*, not power. This would, therefore, omit women from the power equation. However, women controlled indispensable material resources, which helped make the hierarchy more than attentive to their wishes. Further, the male leadership was aware that their efforts to build a denomination—a project in which, aside from their spiritual commitment, they had personal, vested interests—could atrophy if women decided to withdraw their membership, organizations, and resources. This, then, was not mere persuasion or influence; women possessed potential power and were an undeniable force—a latent force but one the Church could not afford to unleash. More importantly, as women continued to meet with bishops and negotiate ministerial appointments, they became increasingly conscious that they possessed this power.

Lessons about the limitations of the authority and power that resided in positions designated exclusively for men was another early understanding that women acquired. It would seem that where official positions are reserved solely for men, men hold dominant power, but the historical actions of AME women challenged this proposition. As we have seen, as early as the 1820s the multitude of rules, policies, and practices that sanctioned only men as preachers, for example, were insufficient to prevent women from functioning in that and other such roles. Beyond the fact that the denomination did not have enough personnel to replace preaching women, if churchmen had attempted to exercise their supposed dominance, they might have forfeited the scores of new members these women attracted—not to mention the contributions of women's groups and their membership in general. Thus the relationship between women, the male hierarchy, and the power needed to accomplish goals was not wholly dependent on position or who held formal authority. It was an active social relationship.

RECIPROCITY-SHIFTING LOCUS

The early experiences of women also taught them that social power is a "give-and-take" phenomenon. The research of Rosabeth Kanter and others has established this to be true also for non–African American organizations of the twentieth century. During the nineteenth century, AME women encountered the dynamic and reciprocal practicalities of power as well. Men held the official positions and with them the authority to make authoritative decisions, but organizational authority without the cooperation of the "rank and file" leaves position holders ineffective. Said another way, the essence of organizations is agreement between members; everyone agrees to adhere to the rules and procedures of the collective. The Church leaders held positions and members implemented their decisions. However, when there was disagreement or disenfranchisement of a significant membership segment, what had seemed a unilateral relationship revealed itself as founded upon reciprocity. Given power sources, the disenfranchised could exercise their power without authority.

In the case of AME women, the male leadership often issued decisions with which the women disagreed, but action was required; the women took action—they *did* nothing. For example, when Church bishops issued a call for a women's missionary magazine, African Methodist women did not activate their network of gender-specific organizations to accomplish the task; they did not respond. It is still unclear why churchwomen disagreed with this decision of the bishops, but the magazine never became a reality in the nineteenth century. Office-holding churchmen had no power to force female members into action. When women possessed numbers, organization, and resources valued by the Church and combined them, the locus of the power relationship shifted. In this instance, the women deliberately withheld their power to accomplish tasks decided upon by Church leaders. This was another means by which women implemented their will.

Yet another way in which the locus, or center, of power could shift within the reciprocal framework could be seen when women proposed alternatives to actions authorized by position holders. Because women possessed the sources of power, their propositions had to be considered despite their lack of official authority.

A decision by the bishops about a missionary assignment to Haiti is a good example of such a shift, as well as of the interactive and reciprocal nature of Church power. Women who had raised funds for the mission to Haiti but refused to release the money to a messenger who was sent to collect it for the Council of Bishops. The women disagreed with the choice of the missionary minister for the assignment and would not act in concert with the episcopal decision. Their inaction shifted the locus from the men holding offices to the women possessing the needed funds. This illustrates that Church power was interactive and interdependent and that results required the efforts of both men and women.

In this episode, the women were not prepared to submit meekly to what seemed to them an obvious error in judgment, even episcopal judgment. The women informed the messenger that they could not release their funds until the bishops reconsidered the appointment. Confident that the bishops would make a wise and correct selection, the women assured the messenger that at such a time they would immediately release their funds.

It was a strategically subtle move. Rather than seize the opportunity produced by the shift in the locus of power to advance a feminist agenda, the women acted on a broader concern, one that reflected awareness of the interconnection between societal patriarchy and institutional racism. First, they did not overtly insist that the men were wrong in their decision but instead issued a polite but assertive request for reconsideration. The women even appeared to defer to the authority of patriarchy by expressing confidence that such a reconsideration would surely produce a wise and correct selection. If so, women promised, the power to accomplish the Church's missionary goals—that is, the funds needed to support the missionary—would be shifted back to the men in decision-making positions.

Second, if AME women had openly challenged the men's authority to assign a minister to Haiti, their actions could have been easily viewed as a threat not only to the gender boundaries of the denomination but also to the patriarchal terrain embedded in the larger white society. African American women were well aware of white society's view of the proper roles of women. Although the AME Church was an independent association and functioned according to cultural definitions of the black community, it also existed within the societal terrain of the United States—terrain that was patriarchal and racist. The slightest indication that churchwomen might cross lines that demarcated gender and racial status could induce whites to intervene in the politics of African American cultural affairs, directly or indirectly. No one was willing to achieve organizational gains for women at the risk of exposing the entire community to its rampant enemy, racism.

Still, AME women lived more immediately within the patriarchy of their own church. To not confront the apparent error of the bishops' decision would have sent what they considered an inappropriate minister to represent a denomination and a people. To those outside the Church and the United States, this could convey the impression that the denomination was incompetent and could imply that its women were passive, making no substantive contributions to Church decisions. The cultural core of African American women's independence would not permit that. They were compelled to take actions that attended to the social struggle against racism while simultaneously forwarding their efforts for gender inclusion. With the knowledge that they possessed a source of power, women finessed both issues as they negotiated with the bishops.

THOSE PREACHING WOMEN

The importance of organizational position is not overshadowed by the fact that power is an interactive phenomenon whose locus can shift. One's position carries the authority of an organization, and AME women fought battles, unsuccessfully for many years, to be included in the Church's formal positions, particularly the ministry. If gender-specific aid groups like the Daughters of Conference were willing to work collaboratively without structural position, and missionary women could avoid serious confrontations within their own organizational sphere, preaching women were not so obliging.

Mrs. Jarena Lee was the first woman to petition the Church for a license to preach, even before the denomination formally existed. It was 1809, and there was no organizational arrangement connecting the several congregations into a single African

Methodist body. Mrs. Lee brought her petition to the flagship congregation in Philadelphia, but she was denied. She returned in 1817, after a connectional body had been formally organized, and received tacit approval for her activities, although social norms and customs did not sanction women speaking in public. Neither were women preachers an established element of the general Methodist tradition.

Sanctioning Jarena Lee to hold prayer meetings in 1817 represented only implicit approval for women preachers, but it set the stage for them to become a constant challenge to the hierarchy and to spearhead changes in the exclusively male composition of the clergy. We have seen in preceding chapters how preaching women as well as other churchwomen across the United States and its territories were exceptionally successful in bringing new members to African Methodism. By 1844, the denomination could no longer ignore the effectiveness of their work. The challenge to license preaching women confronted the Church and deeply affected its governing apparatus.

During the 1844 General Conference, a petition was brought requesting that the body "make provisions for females to preach and exhort." If nothing more, the request was testimony to the fact that Jarena Lee's tacit license to exhort had not been extended to all AME women. The petition was soundly defeated with little discussion. It was as if women were not in the majority in most congregations, did not operate denomination-wide gender-specific organizations, and did not control resources the Church desperately needed. They could not be so easily ignored.

In 1848, another petition for the licensing of preaching women was presented. The hierarchy still had not resolved how to reap the benefits of women's work without altering the churchmen's structural domain and privileges, but conditions were changing. An increasing number of clergymen now had direct experience with women's hermeneutic skills and accomplishments. In addition, some men acknowledged that preaching women were now organized and thereby posed a more serious threat than had been thought. Should these women be alienated and left out, continued Church growth could be negatively affected. Rather than dismiss the petition without comment, this time the men felt compelled to issue a written statement expressing their reasoning for defeating it. An excerpt from the statement read:

> In every sphere of labor, physical and moral, Providence seems to have appropriated the proper laborers. . . . Must the Church, that needs the most manly strength, the most gigantic minds to execute her labors, confide them to those whom nature has fitted for the easier toils of life? . . . When the father of the faithful was to be called and sent into strange and foreign lands to meet frowns of kings and the opposition of foes, was it the gentle, the easy, the confiding Sarah, or was it her lord, her head? . . . When his mighty truths were to be promulgated to a listless world, who was sent forth by heaven's Son, the tender, gentle daughter of Israel, or her more hardy enduring brothers?[1]

So the governing body voted down the 1848 petition to license women preachers. When the question reappeared in 1852, the locus of power still resided with those holding positions of authority, but additional indicators of change were everywhere. On the two previous occasions, four years apart, the General Conference, the highest level of Church governance, had interrupted its regular business to debate what it considered an irregular question. The time and energy of hundreds of delegates had been given to what most men felt was a nonissue—licensed women in the ministry. Few men appeared to support women clergy, but the question continued to require attention at this highest level of the Church.

The men were not willing to license women, but neither were they willing to risk losing the majority of the Church's membership or the organizational potency and resources that women represented. These factors kept delegates at the General Conferences discussing and debating. Even the presiding bishop at the 1852 meeting knew that the stalemate needed to be resolved, though he did not express an opinion in favor of women. He instructed the delegates, "All that I ask is that something distinct may be done that will be satisfactory to all, and the question be put to rest."

After a lengthy discussion, the 1852 gathering defeated the motion by a "large majority." The denominational newspaper, the *Christian Recorder*, reflected the general attitudes of AME men regarding the question of licensing women to preach. The editorial also expressed the sense of threat most delegates felt. A July 1, 1852, editorial read:

> Four years ago this subject of licensing women to preach in the Church came up for consideration before the General Conference in the form of a petition for the Daughters of Zion. It then went so far in their favor that they were granted permission to preach in our churches, but not to receive licenses from the Conference. They again petitioned this [1852] General Conference to grant their *license in all respects as men are licensed, and so to graduate to the highest office in the church.*[2]

The persistent interruption of governance activities to discuss women preachers occurred a fourth time in 1864, and once again the petition was defeated, without comment. But by the time the 1868 General Conference convened, the tenacity and success of preaching women was sufficient to drive the hierarchy into action.

The 1868 meeting was the first since the Civil War. Church membership had expanded by leaps and bounds, with the new "whole church" method of recruitment. Entire congregations of African Americans recently freed from enslavement had united themselves, and the denomination's geographic scope and membership had reached unforeseen heights. There were new sanctuaries, new real estate, and new finances—and women had been indispensable to the phenomenal expansion. Needless to say, women had augmented their power sources as this expansion occurred. Their numerical standing had grown with each new local church. Their network of gender-specific groups had broadened into the South and other territories. As their organizations grew, women had accrued additional material and nonmaterial resources. As the power of women increased, their threat to the organizational authority of delegate churchmen at the 1868 General Conference meeting became more apparent.

Action was required, and a simple negative vote was no longer acceptable; women were too strong. If the men voted to license women to preach, it would surely upset their exclusive hold on official decision making.[3] However, not to authorize preaching women could disrupt women's membership and thus the financial and other material resources that kept the denomination alive. To relinquish privilege, status, and official power is not easy, and AME men found it as difficult as anyone would have when they pondered their dilemma. The 1868 delegates avoided the issue yet again, but they did not just vote "no." The General Conference voted to create a new position exclusively for women—that of stewardess. Though it gave women no license to preach or authority to act on behalf of the denomination, the new position must be seen as a milestone in the struggle for an engendered Church structure.

Previously, there had been no organizational positions for women at all. The stewardess title was a begrudging acknowledgment by the hierarchy that women were a powerful force. Rather than risk a negative consequence by engaging in a struggle with that force, the leadership officially opened the polity to include women. It was a major accomplishment.

In 1872, General Conference delegates and visitors gathered in Nashville, Tennessee. It was the first time African Methodists had convened their highest legislative body in the previously slave-holding South. Among the visitors in Nashville was the nationally famous evangelist Mrs. Amanda Berry Smith. Her extraordinary height and trademark Quaker-style clothing made her highly visible among the assemblage, even as she sat in the balcony. One delegate is reported to have pointed to Mrs. Smith and called out that she was the very embodiment of the threat that preaching women posed to the domain of the all male clergy.

With the stewardess position and Amanda Berry Smith's visibility, "those preaching women" had finally torn the structural fabric of male exclusivity in the African Methodist Episcopal Church, but the stewardess position did not satisfy the totality of women's organizational desires. A stewardess did not require ordination, could not speak for the denomination, had no clerical or ministerial functions, and served under the supervision of male stewards, as well as of the local pastor. Preaching women were particularly dissatisfied and they continued their unauthorized activities. They had so much success in ministering to members and expanding the Church, and received such support from many congregations and pastors, that the denomination would no longer be able to deny a structural place to preaching women.

One significant event precipitated the decision that would occur in 1888: Bishop Henry McNeal Turner ordained Sarah Hughes as a deacon in 1885. He was the presiding bishop of the district that included Sarah Hughes's North Carolina congregation, and she had fulfilled all requirements for ordination. Bishop Turner ordained Mrs. Hughes and she served in her local church. However, as soon as the news reached the Council of Bishops, it convened a meeting. Turner was immediately reprimanded and reminded that the denomination strictly forbade women in any clerical position.[3]

In 1872, the Women's Missionary Mite Society had been organized partly to deflect women's attention away from such ministerial aspirations and toward activities that did not alter the ministry. The Sarah Hughes incident demonstrated that the strategy had been successful only for a time. The preaching women's challenge would not be so easily redirected. In 1888, rather than give women full official license to preach, but in response to new circumstances and pressures from within the ranks of the episcopacy, the boundaries of Church polity were stretched again. The hierarchy subdivided the existing male position of evangelist to establish the office of "female evangelist." This was the only structural place wherein women could be authorized to preach.

The men had made a clever move, authorizing a radical change but preserving their exclusive authority within the clergy. On one hand, they relinquished some power of position by sharing the authority of the preaching license with women. On the other hand, they withheld that authority: the license pertained only to a specific group of women. Women were not to be licensed for any preaching activity outside the evangelist position. Nevertheless, the office of evangelist was yet another achievement in women's struggle toward an engendered Church.

Not long after the Women's Society was called for in 1872, class differences in conjunction with geographic distinctions created such internal tension that the church structure would again have to change in response to the will of women. The issues were not merely differences of opinion, and they were dividing members of the society. The problem arose from the contrast between southern women, whose ancestors had been enslaved, and northern women, whose backgrounds were predominantly among free African Americans. Southern members were the most numerous in the society, but northern women held leadership positions.

The lines of division became clear when churchmen had first issued a call to "bishops' wives" to organize women into the

Missionary Mite Society. This action doubly lessened southern women's representation in the new organization, since in 1872 neither their husbands nor any other southerner held a position in the AME episcopacy. This difference between the women at the origin of their missionary association was aggravated in the course of the association's work.

Since the 1868 stewardess decision, the attention of women had been diverted from achieving a gender-inclusive ministry to working among the hundreds of thousands of destitute, recently freed bondspersons and with the hundreds of new congregations in western territories of the United States. In these locations, women were fully occupied as teachers, class leaders, and stewardesses, and in the Daughters of Conference and other mutual-aid societies. When the Women's Missionary Mite Society was authorized in 1874, it served as an additional organizational basis for women's work. However, the Church was quickly running out of new territories wherein women could work without bumping into the denomination's gender restrictions, particularly the glass ceiling of the clergy. The more-numerous southern women began to focus their energies on missionary activities among southerners and the new western territories, and began to articulate a need for a second women's missionary society for the purpose. There was strong opposition to this idea, but the southern women were determined.

In 1888, when the hierarchy created the post of female evangelist, some northern and southern women were drawn back into the preaching aspect of missionary work, but by 1893 southern women were more committed than ever to organizing a second missionary society specifically for the South and the new western territories. In 1896 (as will be discussed in the next chapter), the will of these women was actualized; the male hierarchy authorized the Women's Home and Foreign Missionary Society, specifically chartered for that work. The structure of the Church had changed for a third time in response to the will of women. In 1900 that polity would make yet another change in response to the presence of women in the Church, establishing the position of deaconess.

Notwithstanding what could be considered too long a delay, the foundation of these changes had been women's possession of numbers, organization, and resources. Women had combined their power sources into a force to be reckoned with by the church hierarchy. Women had effectively made themselves active participants in ministerial decisions that affected their lives, and they had asserted their will in judgments of the episcopal hierarchy. Women were not to be taken for granted, forgotten, or treated lightly. Their latent power represented such a threat that the male leadership was compelled to change the entire denominational structure to accommodate them. Further, women accomplished all of this while sustaining the African Methodist Episcopal Church as a strong social organization, committed to uplifting African American and African people throughout the world. Clearly, AME women had learned the lessons of organizational power and had learned them in a fashion that did not destroy their beloved community. These were the footsteps left by nineteenth-century women, and they were to lead to the election of the first female AME bishop in August 2000.

NOTES

1. Daniel A. Payne, *History of the African Methodist Episcopal Church* (Nashville: African Methodist Sunday School Union, 1891), reprinted 1968 (New York: Johnson Reprint Collection), 300–301.

2. *Christian Recorder*, July 1, 1852 [emphasis supplied].

3. Amanda Berry Smith, *Amanda Smith: The Colored Evangelist* (Chicago: Christian Witness, 1921). The detailed proceedings of the 1868 General Conference have yet to be thoroughly examined.

4. Daniel A. Payne, *Recollections of Seventy Years* (New York: Arno, 1968), 261–64. See also Stephen Ward Angell, *Bishop Henry McNeal Turner and African American Religion in the South* (Knoxville: University of Tennessee Press, 1992), 219.

6

✣

Gendered Spaces:
The Intentionality of Power

One compelling reason to tell the story of AME women is to reclaim the details, significance, and consequences of black churchwomen's collective participation in decision making and in the process of change in their church—to re-explore the first hundred years of AME history, searching for what can be revealed about women and power in the denomination. To complete the task, let us highlight the places and spaces in the Church wherein AME women established themselves.

Collectively, in a century of struggle and accomplishments, women pushed the all-male leadership to relinquish its gender dominance on positions of church structure and to create places for women. But it was the two women's missionary societies that truly exemplified gendered spaces in the denomination. These societies, like most women's organizations, functioned as sheltered arenas wherein women could consolidate their strength, competence, and confidence into a concrete capability to implement their will. These were also arenas in which women worked for women's goals, as well as for a missionary agenda.

It is important to note the illustrative differences between the two missionary societies, including the circumstances of their origins. The dynamics of the missionary spaces constitute a basis from which to review additional examples of black Methodist women's use of power, and to explore the distinctive practices of African American feminism.

BACKGROUND

As we have seen, the Women's Parent Mite Missionary (WPMM) Society was organized in 1874. It was the older of the two women's missionary groups that would exist at the turn of the twentieth century. The origins of WPMM lay in the fund-raising successes of denominational aid groups like the Daughters of Conference that proliferated in the nineteenth century. The network formed by these organizations allowed women to develop such skills as conducting meetings under Robert's Rules of Order. In these havens women nurtured competencies, applied their labor, and gathered material resources that they consistently donated to the Church. The effectiveness of the aid groups was so well known that by 1874 the hierarchy turned to women to provide resources for AME missionary work, which had been faltering.

African Methodist churchmen had attempted as early as the 1830s to finance missionary ministries in Haiti and Santo Domingo, but with little success. The Church's temporary forays into these places could be accomplished only by combining them with normal ministerial assignments in the Caribbean. Even where local interest in forming AME congregations in the islands was strong, the Church was unable to provide sufficient resources to support the work.[1] As the century entered its last quarter, bishops felt that they had let down their sisters and brothers in the Caribbean who were of African descent, that they were derelict in their missionary obligation in comparison to the progress of white denominations. This organizational and racial competitiveness was linked to African Methodism's expanding membership and to the denomination's growing alignment with the values and customs of the larger American society.

When the Emancipation Proclamation was issued in 1862, the federal government felt that Protestant denominations, specifically African American churches, would be useful in the civilizing and socializing tasks needing to be undertaken among the recently freed populations. The proclamation itself, and with it these social responsibilities, was partly the result of southern blacks leaving their enslaved lives to join the liberating Northern forces. A variety of outposts were hurriedly established to teach the "contrabands" the necessary skills for life as wage-earning citizens. Efforts at places like Port Royal, South Carolina, became part of this social experiment, as well as means for maintaining civil order among the African Americans while the Northern forces continued to prosecute the war elsewhere.[2] The AME Church was the first among independent black denominations to be given cooperative responsibilities with white governmental authorities of the military occupation forces. It was a relationship that began early in the war.

In 1862 an AME bishop met for some forty-five minutes with President Abraham Lincoln to inquire whether the president intended to sign a bill abolishing slavery in the District of Columbia. No other African American organization of the period commanded such access at the national level. The white governing establishment saw the AME Church as an accepted and acceptable representative of the black community. It could easily be used to help socialize the thousands of ex-bondspersons now following the Union forces. The military would provide protection for AME ministers for the remainder of the Civil War, and it would become indirectly responsible for successes of the whole-church method of denominational growth.

This apparent, if not real, relationship to the values and customs of the larger American society also brought the independent black organization into closer contact with white denominations. Conditioning the new relationship was an assumption among white social structures, church, and military, that the black denomination shared their broad sociopolitical values, beliefs, and goals. As European American Protestant bodies increased their overseas missionary activities, the AME Church felt somewhat compelled to follow suit. This was true despite the nationalistic identification with the liberation struggles of other groups of African descendants that had motivated the black denomination in its earlier missionary work in Haiti.

As the decade of the 1870s opened, therefore, an entire complex of social, political, national, and cultural factors were in play. The AME hierarchy, feeling itself remiss in its missionary work, began to contemplate ways to remain visible in this important arena of Christian commitment. To salvage its prior efforts and redeem its denominational reputation, as well as what they believed to be the reputation of the African American community, the AME bishops issued an "open letter to the women of the church" calling upon them to apply their organizational skills to missionary goals. It seemed a good idea, in that the recent increases in membership in the South suggested the Church now had a greater potential for accomplishing denominational aspirations. There had been increases in members, real estate, finances, and other indicators of Church wealth. In fact, the rapid expansion by the new whole-church method had stretched resources beyond the organization's capacity to deliver services. The southern expansion also had introduced complexities in the traditional membership base of northeastern free blacks.

As early as 1866 there were more southern members (22,388), than had constituted the entire national AME body just ten years earlier. These recent members contributed $29,601.59 of a total $47,483.76 paid into the denomination's general treasury for 1866. In 1876 there was a two-to-one ratio of southern members to northern ones. Women, as noted previously, accounted for the majority of the new congregants, and for the remainder of the century their numerical share of Church membership would never fall below 55 percent. Despite the numerical and financial strength of southern African Methodists, however, no bishop from the South was elected by the 1864, 1868, or 1872 General Conferences.[3] The leadership was not keeping abreast with changes in Church membership or its geographic distribution.

One new complexity associated with whole-church growth was that the new southern AME members were not converts but practicing Christians transferring from other denominations, mostly white Southern Methodism. These African Americans were familiar with the Protestant tradition and fully understood active membership in local congregations—they were already practicing Christians.

THE WOMEN'S PARENT MITE MISSIONARY SOCIETY

In 1874, when the bishops issued their open letter, they specifically addressed their own wives, not all of the women of the denomination. The letter suggested a latent resentment of women's earlier focus on gender interests; it implicitly accused them of not having supported previous missionary efforts. The episcopal letter reflected all of this even as it invited women to organize a women's missionary society.[4] At a minimum, the tone of the letter mirrored an underappreciation of the Church's changed demographic realities, specifically with respect to its women.

Most wives of bishops resided in northern states, were of free black heritage, and had been raised in literate families capable of maintaining relatively stable lifestyles. Although their social status in American society never approached that of their white counterparts, these seven women were of the bourgeois, the middle class, of African American society and thus did not represent the vast majority of AME women, particularly in the South, where a majority of AME women lived. Nevertheless, the bishops' wives accepted the challenge and called a meeting of women of the denomination. The gathering proposed, and the hierarchy formally authorized, the Women's Parent Mite Missionary Society. No one in the episcopacy or other parts of the ministry could have envisioned the consequences of this additional inclusion of women into the Church's structure.

Late in 1874 the male leadership planned and prepared to commission a certain missionary minister to Port au Prince, Haiti. They had just over a hundred dollars in the missionary treasury, had received another hundred dollars from the general fund, and expected to receive some two to three hundred dollars from the recently created Women's Mite Missionary Society. The bishops, having made their ministerial selection for the assignment, sent the male secretary of the Missionary Department to collect the funds from the women. In an episode that has been discussed earlier, the women did not approve of the selected minister and refused to transfer their money. Without support from women, the men were powerless to implement their own decision. The departmental secretary returned to the Council of Bishops empty-handed and reported the women's position. There was much discussion among the bishops and public debate in the Church's newspaper, the *Christian Recorder*.

The women's prior experience with decision making in their denomination suggests that the women leaders were acting on behalf of the entire missionary society and with complete awareness of the significance of their challenge to the bishops. It had been fifty-eight

years since Daughters of Conference groups had been organized
and women had learned much about how their church functioned,
how to organize within that system, and how to negotiate effectively using the leverage offered by their sources of power. In February 1876 the women leaders called a meeting of the society's full
membership to discuss the bishops' new appointment. The society
had $637.29 to contribute, once it agreed that the bishops had
made a suitable ministerial selection.

In their normal fashion, after the reconsideration and the change
of the missionary minister, the women convened their members, approved of the new episcopal selection, and turned over their donation to the Missionary Department. However, the report of the
WPMM Society to the General Conference in the summer of 1876
did not refer to this challenge to the male decision makers. Rather,
official written documents maintained an organizationally support-
ive tone "We only want for you, the heads of our church, to get the
matter thoroughly started that we may be the better able to work."[5]
The incident merits this further discussion as evidence of women using their power but not destroying their church.

The male leadership had expanded church structure to form the
WPMM and to draw upon women's financial and other material
resources. A structural space had been created to engage the labor,
skills, organization, and resources of women in goals set by the hierarchy. However, even from its beginnings the gender-specific society was also a place where women refined their ability to unite
and use their sources of power within the Church. The society was
the first authorized denomination-wide organizational space in
which women could negotiate among themselves before publicly
expressing a group position. Within the boundaries of the society,
women enhanced the quality of their participation and thus further inserted themselves into decision-making processes.

However, the society also, reflected internal divisions that existed
in the denomination as a whole. By the final quarter of the nineteenth century, as noted, the Northeast was no longer the Church's
geographical center of membership or financial support. Southerners
accounted for the largest number of African Methodists and were
the denomination's main financial contributors. That few Church
leaders were from the South became increasingly intolerable to them.
This was particularly true in the women's missionary society.

WOMEN'S HOME AND FOREIGN MISSIONARY SOCIETY

Differences in socioeconomic classifications began to fracture the Church and the women's missionary work. These differences manifested themselves as geographic divisions. Although the economic standard of life of southern blacks was lower than that of their northern sisters and brothers, their financial contributions to the Church were not dramatically lower. For example, over the seventeen months between November 1878 and April 1880, women from the Northeast raised and donated $1,021.80; Southern women—who had been members of the denomination for merely ten years, compared to northern women's thirty-eight—were responsible for more than half, $639.47 of the total.

Even the collection of the $627.29 that women eventually donated to the Church's Haitian mission had a geographic dimension. Southern women—recent members, newly freed from enslavement, and in a highly precarious economic situation—provided a remarkable $184.06.[6] In all, southern women, most recently exposed to the organizational norms of AME life, were already firmly on the road to carrying their full share of financial responsibility in the Church.

Also visible among women in the missionary association were the outward indicators of social class that reflected the geographical differences within the general African American population. For the most part, the community's symbols of privilege and social acceptability were those of European American lifestyles and therefore rare and hard to obtain for African Americans. Free black heritage, light-brown to yellowish skin color, relative economic stability, and some degree of formal education were indicators of social class differences in the black community. These indicators were significant, because they usually suggested a close relationship to the influence of privileged whites. Such a relationship could provide African Americans a protective screen behind which they could find opportunities for achievement.[7]

Most officers of the older Women's Parent Mite Missionary Society—wives of Church bishops—possessed these social class characteristics. The concentration of these indicators among the women leaders, the absence of southern women in positions of leadership, and the concomitant increase in membership and

support of southern women in the WPMM Society created feelings of discrimination among women of the South.

One southern member familiar with these realities captured the
feelings of tension and discrimination based on social class differences. Of northern women she wrote that they had traditionally
"been of the highest type, many of them wives, mothers, sisters
and daughters of the high dignitaries of our church." In African
American society and the AME Church, "high" connoted the social indicators mentioned above. Notably, the author described
the Society's southern women not as of "high type" but as "our
most excellent workers."[8]

As activities of the WPMM Society proceeded, southern women
became increasingly restless and dissatisfied. In September 1893,
a delegation of southern women traveled to South Bend, Indiana,
to petition the bishop responsible for the Church's General Board
of Missions, the administrative unit in charge of all missionary
work. The women wanted to establish a second society for the
"thousands of women in the south and west who desired to work
for missions."[9] They wished neither to divert the denomination's
missionary endeavor nor to destroy the denomination but to preserve both. To do so, the women knew, they needed a direct link
with someone who held a position of authority—a bishop.

The delegation was attempting a subtle exercise of organizational power in aligning its sources of informal power with formal
authority. African Methodist women had learned well the lessons
of the sources and use of power. Not only were they proposing a
second missionary society for women of the South and West, but
they had elected to join forces with the first southerner elected to
the episcopacy since the Civil War. The women traveled to Indiana
to petition this man to support them. It was a timely move.

Henry McNeal Turner, the first post–Civil War southerner to become a bishop in the AME Church, had been elected only after the
northern-dominated leadership had rejected as unqualified several
southern candidates, on several previous occasions. It was only after
southern delegates to the 1880 General Conference caucused and
formed a voting bloc that a candidate from south of the Mason-
Dixon Line was elected bishop. Turner was that minister, and he understood well the quasi-geographic, social-class discriminations that
southern women were experiencing. Turner too had endured the pa-

tronizing paternalism of northerners toward southerners, but he was an assertive and decisive man, prepared to advance African Methodism wherever people of African descent lived. For that purpose he was willing to use all available resources.[10]

Bishop Turner, then, was an appropriate choice for southern women in a bid for support of their second missionary society. He was a southerner, he was progressive in attitude and action; further, it was he who, contrary to Church practice and policy, had ordained a woman as deacon in 1885. Consequently he was severely reprimanded. By 1893, southern women knew that here was the man who was the most likely of all men in authority to be willing to confront the exclusively male bastion of formal Church leadership. If the women could demonstrate a commonality of interest with him, Turner might be convinced to align his official power with the missionary women's numerical strength, organization, and resources. The 1893 delegation of southerners from the WPMM Society was well prepared as they traveled to Indiana.[11]

Beyond issues of regional loyalties and class discrimination, the women had an added argument with which to persuade the bishop to support their plan. They intended that the focus of the second society would be to provide resources for the much-needed work among African Americans in southern states. These women had personal experience with the abject poverty and social needs of blacks in the region. Conditions had worsened since the withdrawal of military support for Reconstruction. The retreat from the guarantees of African Americans' rights of citizenship had allowed the resurgence of white control of southern politics. The political return to the rule of white supremacy had been reinforced by frequent and violent attacks against blacks. In addition, the pervasive allocation of social resources and privilege based on white skin meant that southern black citizens had very little negotiating space for self-advocacy. The situation was a threat to the survival of the African American community; it demanded focused attention. Southern AME women were sure that Bishop Turner understood these dynamics well enough to see the need for a missionary society. They felt that his compassionate understanding as well as his political savvy would move him to join their petition to create a second society in the Church.[12]

Southern women had positioned themselves and their power sources well. The bishop had already demonstrated his willingness to cross formal boundaries with regard to women. He was directly in charge of the Church's General Board of Missions. He had been born and raised in the South. But equally important was the fact that Bishop Henry McNeal Turner had an agenda that converged with that of the women. Turner wanted to increase the pool of resources available to the denomination for missionary activities, specifically to carry out expansion work that he began in southern Africa.

The Indiana conversation between the southern delegation and Bishop Turner was a success. They envisioned a society whose outreach and fund-raising would focus on missionary work in the United States as well as designated overseas locations. Half of the money that women raised would remain in the Church's Annual Conference structure and be used for work among the black population in southern states. The remaining half would be reported to the general missionary department under Bishop Turner and be made available for foreign missionary endeavors. The authority of the bishop and the sources of power possessed by southern women had combined in an unbeatable coalition.[13]

The Council of Bishops agreed to the collaborative plan. However, details of the council's debate and discussion on this issue are not known. The men probably agreed because they were powerless to stand against it. Women represented the majority of denominational membership; southerners of both genders were also in the majority; Turner held a position of authority and was now supporting southern women who possessed the sources of power and were now committing themselves to produce more resources, organization, and numbers for the Church. The Bishop's council was unlikely to have opposed such a combination.

At the 1896 General Conference, the new Women's Home and Foreign Missionary (WHFM) Society was established, ultimately, under the supervision of the bishop of general missions. There was much opposition to this second society for women, opposition outside the council and within the larger body of delegates to the General Conference. The opposition, which was particularly strong among men who held other leadership positions in the hierarchy, would continue for some two generations, into the twentieth century. However, the opposition was not able to offset the power sources of southern women, particularly combined with episcopal authority. African Methodist women had learned how to make themselves indispensable and to make themselves a force capable of overcoming opposition.

NOTES

1. See Jualynne E. Dodson "Encounters in the African Atlantic World: The African Methodist Episcopal Church in Cuba" in *Between Race and Empire: African Americans and Cubans before the Cuban Revolution,* ed. Lisa Brock and Digna Castaneda Fuertes (Philadelphia: Temple University Press, 1998).

2. Willie Lee Rose, *Rehearsal for Reconstruction: The Port Royal Experiment* (Indianapolis: Bobbs-Merrill, 1964).

3. Benjamin Arnett, *Budget of 1885–86, Ninth African Methodist Episcopal Church* (unpublished, 1886), 297, and *The Budget of 1904* (Philadelphia: Rev. E. W. Lampton and Rev. J. H. Collett, 1904), 161, 173–74. See also Jualynne E. Dodson, *Collective Power: Women and the AME Church* (Ph.D. diss., University of California, Berkeley, 1984), 47.

4. Richard R. Wright, *Centennial Encyclopaedia of the African Methodist Episcopal Church* (Philadelphia: AME Book Concern, 1916).

5. AME Church, *Sixteenth Session and the Fifteenth Quadrennial Session of the General Conference of the African Methodist Episcopal Church* (unpublished, 1876), 221; AME Church, *Third Annual Meeting of the General Missionary Board* (unpublished, 1882), 290–93.

6. Wright, *Centennial Encyclopaedia,* 320.

7. Andrew Billingsley, *Black Families in White America* (Englewood Cliffs, N.J.: Prentice-Hall, 1968), 196.

8. Reverdy C. Ransom, *Preface to History of African Methodist Episcopal Church* (Nashville, Tenn.: AME Sunday School Union, 1950), 188–92; Sara J. Hatcher Duncan, *Progressive Missions in the South and Addresses with Illustrations and Sketches of Missionary Workers and Ministers and Bishops' Wives* (Atlanta: Franklin, 1906), 143.

9. Ransom, *Preface.*

10. See Stephen Ward Angell, *Bishop Henry McNeal Turner and African-American Religion in the South* (Knoxville: University of Tennessee Press, 1992).

11. Daniel A. Payne, *Recollections of Seventy Years* (New York: Arno, 1968), 261–64.

12. AME Church, *Journal of the Nineteenth Session and Eighteenth Quadrennial Session of the General Conference* (1888), 180–287, esp. 198.

13. Angell, *Bishop Henry McNeal Turner*, 219.

7

✞

A Pinnacle of Power
to Close the Century:
Sara Hatcher Duncan

I am because we are;
we are, therefore I am.

—African Proverb

In 1900, Sara Hatcher Duncan was appointed president of the Women's Home and Foreign Missionary Society of the AME Church. Sara Duncan was the personification of the goals nineteenth-century African Methodist women had set for themselves and struggled to achieve. She was the free-born child of an ex-slave, a southerner; she had been formally educated; within the limitations of the economic conditions of southern African Americans, her status was economically stable; and she held active membership in most social and civic associations that the state of Alabama allowed black women to form. She was also a wife, a foster mother, a trained teacher, and a caring neighbor. She was active in Church organizations and regularly contributed articles on the conditions of black women to newspapers and magazines of the period. In 1906 she even published her own book, *Progressive Missions in the South*. By all accounts and standards set for mature African American women, Sara Hatcher Duncan was "a race woman."

The "race woman" was a nineteenth-century ideal that captured the behavior, attitudes, and objectives of adult African American women who had achieved true womanhood. In the abstract as well as the particular, the race woman, or woman for the race, epitomized the role black women prescribed for themselves as they grew out of the mind-set of slavery and created social institutions and organizations to help improve the condition of the African American community. The goals of race women emphasized a collective uplifting through individual achievement. Paula Giddings's *When and Where I Enter* is a perceptive exploration of this idea. Individuals who benefited from opportunities of freedom after the Civil War were expected to help lift other African Americans up the ladder of success, thereby ensuring the social improvement and achievement of the entire community.[1]

The close of the nineteenth century and opening of the twentieth required the collective approach and special characteristics of race women. In 1896, the U.S. Supreme Court issued its ruling in the case of *Plessy vs. Ferguson*. This monumental decision legalized racial segregation of blacks and whites throughout the United States and all its territories, such as Cuba, Puerto Rico, Guam, the Philippines, and Hawaii. The decision effectively took back all the civil rights earned by African Americans since the Civil War and established a pattern of rigid, segregated national life that continued for more than seventy years, deep into the twentieth century.

In addition, daily lynchings and other violent manifestations of white racist attitudes and behavior reinforced the impact of *Plessy v. Ferguson*. These virulent forms of racism were aggravated by the 1915 release of D. W. Griffith's film *Birth of a Nation*. Herein were images—sanctioned by the president of the United States, and based upon distortions of African Americans and their history in the life of the nation—that justified the idea and practice of white supremacy. Sara Hatcher Duncan and other black women wisely aspired to be race women in order to fight the racism and injustice of such institutional forces.

The black community universally felt that only collective success could counter white society's hostility. Committed women whose lives personified devotion to uplifting, the race would be important weapons in combatting the prevailing attitudes asserting African American inferiority. These were late-nineteenth-century attitudes rationalized by theories of social Darwinism, popular during the period.

As the nineteenth century closed, black women, who continued to build strong social organizations, assumed responsibility for defending the moral integrity of their gender, demanding justice for their sisters of the race, and insisting upon the cultural prerogatives of their community. The race woman ideas that closed the century are compatible with contemporary views of "womanist" identity. "Womanism" refers to the socially constructed and distinct set of attitudes and behaviors that constitute feminist gender identity for African American women of the United States. Introduced by Alice Walker and adopted by other writers, theologians, social scientists, and scholars, the concept of "womanist" is congruent with the nineteenth-century idea of race woman. Both concepts can be used to explore the life of Sara Hatcher Duncan as the epitome of African Methodist women's power-related accomplishments. As president of the WHFM, Sara Duncan was the embodiment of both concepts, just as Rev. Vashti Murphy McKenzie, the first female bishop of the AME Church, stands at the opening of the twenty-first century as the culmination of women's power accomplishments in her own time.

Unwavering commitment to the creation of a church community that could expand social alternatives for all blacks was a womanist idea that resonated with the goals of nineteenth-century AME women. The forerunners of Sara Hatcher Duncan would have been pleased with the denominational positions that had been opened for women by 1900. They also would have been gratified to see who Sara Hatcher Duncan was and how she chose to interact with AME churchmen. Sara's behavioral approach met race woman womanist criteria. She was committed to the survival and wholeness of an entire people, female and male. She was married to Robert H. Duncan. She knew herself as having evolved from the collective, the socio-cultural community of African Americans, specifically the African Methodism of Alabama. Her life and her work were rooted in the world of black women, specifically with the women's missionary societies of her church. She was responsible, in charge, serious, and unafraid to speak out for women in gendered spaces that the power of AME women had carved out. She continued to work with men of the Church even when their behavior did not seem to merit cooperation. Overcoming severe odds, Sara Hatcher Duncan led the second women's missionary association, the Home and Foreign Missionary Society, to ascendancy by the close of the nineteenth century. All of these attributes characterize the African American feminist, race woman, and womanist. Sara Duncan was the personification of these characteristics. She fully represents the black women's creation of social organization and self-identity within African Methodism.

Sara J. Hatcher was born on October 5, 1869, in Cahaba, Alabama, the youngest of four children. Her father, S. George Hatcher, born into slavery, now made his living in grocery and liquor retail, having abandoned the blacksmith trade taught to him by his father. The elder Hatcher had been an enslaved tradesman who had hired out his time and that of his sons. Sara's mother (and George's third wife), Eliza English, was of mulatto heritage. She died a year and one month after the birth of Sara, their fourth child. Mrs. Sara J. Morgan raised the baby as one of her five foster children.

Despite the heritage of enslavement, Sara's family enjoyed a relatively stable and secure income. They were nothing like rich, but they had sufficient financial resources and political connections to enrich Sara's childhood. Little Sara helped her grandfather with his postal duties in Cahaba, Alabama. Jordan Hatcher, who had obtained the position of postmaster of Cahaba after the Civil War, encouraged Sara's assistance. He also had been a member of the 1868 Alabama constitutional convention, as well as a schoolteacher. By her own account, therefore, until she was twelve years old, Sara's education was by way of her grandfather or other tutorial instruction.[2] She attended public school thereafter, continuing her education at the Presbyterian Knox Academy of Selma, Alabama. This level of formal education was beyond that of most African Methodists of the period, particularly southern women, and it would help elevate Sara to the pinnacle she would occupy at the close of the century.

In 1889, Sara married Robert H. Duncan of Rome, Georgia, where she resided for some seven years. She was involved in her local church, an involvement that had begun as early as her twelfth year. The new Mrs. Duncan served as principal of the Spring Street School and engaged in missionary work for the North Alabama Annual Conference of the AME Church. In 1893, Sara returned to

Selma to care for her aging father. This was the year that southern AME women met with Bishop Henry McNeal Turner in South Bend, Indiana, to communicate their unwavering resolve to form a second, more southern-oriented AME women's missionary society. This second society was the organizational entity through which Sara Duncan would carry out her womanist work.

The Women's Home and Foreign Missionary Society was more than the second women's missionary organization of the Church. Its existence was specifically a result of the insistence of churchwomen who had begun to perceive class-based inequities within their denomination. Southern women led the effort because it was they who felt excluded from positions of authority in the older, northern-controlled Women's Parent Mite Missionary Society. The creation of a second society was meant to respond to the southern women's critique and to keep the totality of women's activities within the governance of the Church. However, the demands of these women were not well received by many of the men who held positions of authority. The second society was created only over great opposition, and the men appointed a northern woman, Mrs. Lillian Thurman, as its first general superintendent. Mrs. Thurman was a capable leader but not a southerner. She resigned the position after six months of service. In 1897, Sara Hatcher Duncan was appointed acting general superintendent and began her work. She now had the position and opportunity to develop the society and its work with a specifically southern tilt.

In August of 1898, Sara gave her first report to the general secretary of the Council of Presiding Elders. This was only two years after the infamous *Plessy vs. Ferguson* decision, but already events suggested that the black community faced a long battle to regain its civil rights. Sara would not forget that battle, but she was primarily devoted to her contest against the sexism of the AME Church. Consistent with characteristic womanist's awareness of the need to develop and support community, Sara began her report by articulating her lifetime involvement with and commitment to the Church. However, this affirmation was also a strategic accommodation to the churchmen who held official position:

> Now, my brethren, I have endeavored to hold up the missionary banner of the Church since my appointment, and I have had great pride in the same; first, because the honor conferred is the first in

the history of the Church to be given a woman of the South[;] . . . secondly, because I have felt that from my earliest existence, . . . that "there was a destiny that shaped my end." And having been reared in the African Methodist Episcopal church, and taught to be a missionary from my earliest childhood.[3]

Sara was presenting herself and the work of the society as committed to the "banner of the church" rather than to an attempt to function independently. This surely reassured the men as to the security of their leadership positions.

But a characteristic of womanist identity that Sara personified is a serious willingness to speak out for women. This attribute did not allow her to acquiesce in, and be silent about, the lack of cooperation from presiding elders and ministers assigned to work with the new society. Further, she had an organizational ground from which to launch the critique that immediately followed. It mattered not that this was her first report to the hierarchy. Sara's position as president of the WHFM had been made possible by years of struggle by thousands of churchwomen before her. She was prepared to be unyielding in holding the leadership accountable for their lack of cooperation. Sara boldly spoke for women in her well-founded accusation:

> But, my brethren, how often in the hours of disappointment, solitude, want and deprivation have I wondered if I had the sympathy of the P.E. [presiding elder] and ministers who should be my standard bearers. . . ?
>
> [T]he disappointments came in numbers of ways. When a P.E. would get me to take up his district to work through I would look to him, as chief, to notify the ministers of my coming, and some engagement made for my board. Then the ministers in some places have instead of preparing for me, left the place, not even telling the people of my coming, and some invited minister of another denomination having charge of the Church.[4]

These had been grave insults, and Sara Hatcher Duncan would not allow them to go unrecorded and unprotested.

Sara Duncan was an informed woman and knew the successes of her church as well as its lines of stress and tension. She would not personally engage the question of ordaining women, but neither would she allow men who feared women's motives in missionary work to intimidate her. At this 1898 meeting she began with an emphasis on the collective and continued to detail the individual perspective, with herself as an example. She concluded with a ringing challenge:

> And, brethren, if you have any ministers in your district who seem to have so much jealousy in them against the women concerning their work, tell them that we are not trying to take their pulpits; for my part I have studied the history of the Church since my connection with the same, when only eleven years old. I have studied its laws seventeen years and, had I been aspiring for the pulpit, could have taken an examination for elder's orders ten years ago.[5]

This was Sara's first report to her superiors, yet she had no problem speaking truth. To supplement her voice, she launched a missionary newspaper, *Missionary Searchlight*. It had a gender orientation, a focus on women interested in missionary and missions work. She began it in 1898, and the next two general conferences adopted it.

Like many who had been raised in the race woman, womanist traditions of the nineteenth-century AME Church, Sara Duncan was prolific in her written addresses, speeches, and greetings to various assemblies. In these, she represented well her inheritance as a race woman. On the need of inclusiveness for community survival, she wrote, "We are striving to save the children, both boys and *girls*" (my emphasis). She wrote on the need for women to be forthright in their self-expression: "Women must write, speak, sing and do everything whereby those of our race may receive inspiration."

Sara knew that as a group women were oppressed, but she was equally clear that black women were doubly oppressed, as both women and African Americans. She addressed this double jeopardy in a response to an article by a Mrs. Green, a European American woman of Washington, Georgia. Green had declared on a train that she felt much safer in the sleeper car with a southern white man than in the "colored" section of the day coach. Sara Duncan's response centered on the false privilege of being white—an African American woman would be little safer in the sleeper car with a southern white man than in the day coach. "Now, if Mrs. Green had been a colored woman she would have had the same fear had her fellow-passenger been a white man, . . . for the world over, men are men; woman is simply a woman with him, and he cares not for the color of the skin. They [white women] have no opportunity to know as much of this as we[,] . . . for they are not placed in the same position.[6]

Despite her gifts and skills, the accomplishments of Sara J. Hatcher Duncan were not totally her own doing. She followed a long list of African Methodist women, many more prominent than she but most, like her, completely unheralded. Together they forged organizational space in the AME Church for Sara's late nineteenth- and early twentieth-century opportunities. Those pioneering women would have been delighted with the content and style of Sara's work.

They would have known that the mere ability to command a formal audience with male authorities of the Church was a hard-won achievement, not to be wasted in insignificant accolades or inappropriate gratitude. The pioneering women would have known that to be a black woman required community as well as independence. They would have known that all women lived under men but that black women lived under all whites as well. Sara Hatcher Duncan was an excellent representative of that for which AME women before her had struggled—she was a pinnacle of women's power in their church.

NOTES

1. For a full discussion of nineteenth-century race women, see Paula Giddings, *When and Where I Enter: The Impact of Black Women on Race and Sex in America*, 2d ed. (New York: Morrow, 1996).

2. Sara J. Duncan, *Progressive Missions in the South: An Address with Illustrations and Sketches of Missionary Workers and Ministers and Bishops' Wives* (Atlanta: Franklin, 1906).

3. Duncan, *Missions*, 64.

4. Duncan, *Missions*, 66.

5. Duncan, *Missions*, 70.

6. Duncan, *Missions*, 337.

Bibliography

ANONYMOUS AME MATERIALS

The African Wesleyan Methodist Episcopal Church [known as the Bridge Street Church], New York. 1980.

Christian Recorder, July 1, 1852.

Christian Recorder, new series, no. 103, vol. 9, no. 509, March 18, 1871.

Christian Recorder, February 23, 1886.

Christian Recorder, April 2, 1886.

Christian Recorder, July 7, 1886.

Christian Recorder, December 3, 1903.

First Annual Report of the Board of Managers of the Shelter for Aged and Infirm Colored Persons of Baltimore City. Unpublished, 1883.

Fourteenth Annual Report of the National Association for the Relief of Destitute Colored Women and Children. Washington, D.C.: O. H. Reed, 1877.

The Red Book of Houston: A Compendium of Social, Professional, Religious, Educational, and Industrial Interests of Houston's Colored Population. Houston: Sotex, c. 1915.

Second Annual Report of the Board of Managers of the Shelter for Aged and Infirm Colored Persons of Baltimore City. Unpublished, 1884.

Statistical Inquiry into the Condition of the People of Colour of the City and Districts of Philadelphia. Philadelphia: Kite and Walton, 1849.

"Vital Questions: Our Missionary Department." *Christian Recorder,* December 3, 1903.

ARCHIVAL AME REFERENCES

African Methodist Episcopal Church. *Big Bethel African Methodist Episcopal Church: A Century of Progress and Christian Service.* Atlanta, 1968.

———. *Fifteenth Quadrennial Session of the General Conference of the African Methodist Episcopal Church.* 1872.

———. *Journal of Proceedings of the Eighty-first Session of the Philadelphia Annual Conference of the African Methodist Episcopal Church.* 1897.

———. *Minutes of the Eleventh Session of the East Arkansas Annual Conference.* c. 1910.

———. *Minutes of the New Jersey Annual Conference of the African Methodist Episcopal Church for 1879.* 1879.

———. *Minutes and Reports of the Fifth Quadrennial Convention of the Women's Parent Mite Missionary Society Held in Quinn Chapel, Chicago, November 9th–13th, 1911.* 1911.

———. "Probationers' Book 1845–1881, African Methodist Episcopal Church." Baltimore, 1845.

———. *Sixteenth Session and the Fifteenth Quadrennial Session of the General Conference of the African Methodist Episcopal Church.* 1876.

———. *Souvenir Children's Day 1895.* Nashville, Tenn., 1894.

———. *Third Annual Meeting of the General Missionary Board.* 1882.

Logsdon, Joseph A. "The Rev. Archibald J. Carey and the Negro in Chicago Politics." Master's thesis, University of Chicago, Department of History, Chicago, 1961.

Methodist Episcopal Church. "Minutes of Class Meeting." Minutes circa 1838–41, 1850, undated, 1854–56, AME Church Records, folder 4, box 1, Moorland-Spingarn Research Center, Howard University, Washington, D.C., 1838.

———. "Board of Trustees Meeting of Union Bethel Church." Minutes circa 1838–41, 1850, undated, 1854–56, AME Church Records, folder 4, box 1, Moorland-Spingarn Research Center, Howard University, Washington, D.C., 1841.

———. "Minutes of the Quarterly Conference of Union Bethel African Methodist Episcopal Church." Minutes c. 1838–41, 1850, undated, 1854–56, AME Church Records, folder 4, box 1, Moorland-Spingarn Research Center, Howard University, Washington, D.C., 1854.

———. "Constitution of the Sinking Fund Association." Deposit Book at Freedman's Saving and Trust for Sinking Fund, Manuscript and Journal, Metropolitan AME Church Records, folders 6 and 7, box 1, Moorland-Spingarn Research Center, Howard University, Washington, D.C., 1871.

Payne, Daniel A. *Morris Brown*. Samuel Hopkins Atlanta University Archives, Countee Culleen Collection, Giles folder, n.d.

———. "Journal." Manuscript, Daniel Papers, Moorland-Spingarn Research Center, Howard University, Washington, D.C., 1877–1878.

Perry, Grace Naomi. "The Education Work of the African Methodist Episcopal Church prior to 1900." Master's thesis, Howard University, Washington, D.C., 1948.

Rush, Benjamin. *Short Account of the Rise and Progress of the African Methodist Episcopal Zion Church in America*. New York, 1843.

Simms Family. "Register of Members of Union Bethel African Methodist Episcopal Church." Manuscript journal, Simms Family Papers, box 1, Moorland-Spingarn Research Center, Howard University, Washington, D.C., 1839.

———. "Obituary Martha Ann Simms." Manuscript, Simms Family Papers, box 1, Moorland-Spingarn Research Center, Howard University, Washington, D.C., c. 1896.

Swan, Robert J. "The Black Church in Brooklyn." In *An Introduction to the Black Contribution to the Development of Brooklyn*, unpublished manuscript, New York, 1977.

Tanner, Benjamin Tucker. *An Outline of Our History and Government for African Methodist Churchmen*. Philadelphia, 1884.

———. *The Dispensations in the History of the Church and the Interregnums*. 1898.

Tanner, C. M. *Reprint of the First Edition of the Discipline of the African Methodist Episcopal Church*. Atlanta, 1917.

Trotter, Donald F. "A Study of Authority and Power in the Structure and Dynamics of the Southern Baptist Convention." Ph.D. dissertation, Southern Baptist Theological Seminary, Louisville, Ky., 1962.

———. "Life and Works of Henry McNeal Turner." Manuscript, Henry McNeal Turner Papers, folder 1, boxes 1–106, Moorland-Spingarn Research Center, Howard University, Washington, D.C., n.d.

Walker, Clarence Earl. *A Rock in a Weary Land: A History of the African Methodist Episcopal Church during the Civil War and Reconstruction*. Ph.D. dissertation, University of California, Berkeley, 1976.

Wills, David. "Aspects of Social Thoughts in the African Methodist Episcopal Church, 1884–1910." Ph.D. dissertation, Harvard University, Cambridge, Massachusetts, 1975.

PUBLISHED AME REFERENCES

African Methodist Episcopal Church. "Board of Trustees: Minutes 1846–1867, Bethel African Methodist Episcopal Church." Baltimore: n.p., 1846–1867.

——. *Catalogue of Wilberforce University for Academic Year 1880–1881.* Xenia, Ohio: Xenia Gazette, 1881.

——. *Centennial Historical Souvenir of "Mother" Bethel African Methodist Episcopal Church.* Philadelphia: Historical Society, 1916.

——. *Class Leader's Book of Members of the Bethel African Methodist Episcopal Church.* Baltimore, 1852.

——. *The Doctrine and Discipline of the African Methodist Episcopal Church.* 2d rev. ed. Philadelphia: n.p., 1832.

——. *The Doctrine and Discipline of the African Methodist Episcopal Church.* 19th rev. ed. Philadelphia: AME Book Concern, 1888.

——. *First Annual Report of the Parent Home and Foreign Missionary Society of the African Methodist Episcopal Church.* Terre Haute, Ind.: C. W. Brown, 1880.

——. *Journal of the Eighteenth Session and Seventeenth Quadrennial Session of the General Conference of the African Methodist Episcopal Church in the World.* Philadelphia: Rev. James C. Embry, 1884.

——. *Journal of the Nineteenth Session and Eighteenth Quadrennial Session of the General Conference of the African Methodist Episcopal Church in the World.* Philadelphia: Rev. James C. Embry, 1888.

——. *Journal of Proceedings of the Eighty-second Session of the Philadelphia Annual Conference of the African Methodist Episcopal Church.* Philadelphia: AME Publishing House, 1898.

——. *Journal of Proceedings of the Fourth Quadrennial Convention of the Women's Parent Mite Missionary Society of the African Methodist Episcopal Church.* Philadelphia: AME Publishing House, 1908.

——. *Journal of Proceedings of the Twenty-fifth Session of the New Jersey Annual Conference.* Philadelphia: AME Publishing House, 1897.

——. *Journal of Proceedings of the Thirty-third Session of the South Carolina Annual Conference.* Philadelphia: AME Publishing House, 1897.

——. *Minute Book of United Daughters of Tapaico, 1837–1847.* Philadelphia: Mother Bethel, 1837.

——. *Minutes of the Baltimore Annual Conference of the African Methodist Episcopal Church.* Baltimore: James Young, 1859.

——. *Minutes of the Eighteenth Session of the California Annual Conference of the African Methodist Episcopal Church.* San Francisco: Edward C. Hughes, 1885.

——. *Minutes of the Fifteenth Session of the South Carolina Annual Conference of the African Methodist Episcopal Church.* Beaufort, S.C.: Crescent, 1879.

——. *Minutes of the Fourth Session after Division of the Columbia, South Carolina Conference of the African Methodist Episcopal Church.* Charleston, S.C.: News and Courier, 1882.

———. *Minutes of the New England Annual Conference of the African Methodist Episcopal Church*. New Bedford, Mass.: Benjamin Lindsey, 1852.

———. *Minutes of the New England Annual Conference of the African Methodist Episcopal Church in America*. New Bedford, Mass.: E. Anthony, 1859.

———. *Minutes of the New England Annual Conference of the African Methodist Episcopal Church in America*. New Bedford, Mass.: 1862.

———. *Minutes of the New England Annual Conference of the African Methodist Episcopal Church in America*. New Bedford, Mass.: E. Anthony, 1866.

———. *Minutes of the Nineteenth Session of the West Tennessee Conference*. Nashville, Tenn.: AME Church Sunday School Union, 1895.

———. *Minutes of the Second Session of the Columbia, South Carolina Conference of the African Methodist Episcopal Church*. Columbia, S.C.: W. B. McDaniel, 1879–1880.

———. *Minutes of the Seventy-fifth Session of the Philadelphia Annual Conference*. Philadelphia: Allen, 1891.

———. *Minutes of the Seventh Annual Session of the South Carolina Conference before Division of the African Methodist Episcopal Church*. Columbia, S.C.: J. Denny, 1871.

———. *Minutes of the Tenth Session before Division of the South Carolina Annual Conference of the African Methodist Episcopal Church*. Columbia, S.C.: Republican, 1874.

———. *Minutes of the Tenth Session after Division* [sic] *of the New Jersey Annual Conference of the African Methodist Episcopal Church*. Philadelphia: Christian Recorder, 1883.

———. *Minutes of the Thirteenth Session of the North Carolina Annual Conference of the African Methodist Episcopal Church in the United States of America*. Wilmington, N.C.: S. G. Hall, 1880.

———. *Minutes of the Thirteenth Session of the West Tennessee Annual Conference*. Clarksville, Tenn.: W. P. Titus, 1889.

———. *Minutes of the Thirty-fifth Annual Conference for the New York District of the African Methodist Episcopal Church Held in Bethel Church Second Street, New York City*. New York: John W. Zuille, 1855.

———. *Minutes of the Thirty-fourth Session of the New England Annual Conference of the African Methodist Episcopal Church*. Philadelphia: Christian Recorder, 1885.

———. *Minutes of the Twelfth Session before Division of the South Carolina Annual Conference of the African Methodist Episcopal Church*. Charleston, S.C.: Walker, Evans, and Cogswell, 1876.

———. *Minutes of the Twentieth New England Annual Conference*. Providence, R.I.: A. Crawford Greene, 1872.

———. *Minutes of the Twenty-fourth Session of the New England Annual Conference of the African Methodist Episcopal Church.* Providence, R.I.: A. Crawford Greene, 1875.

———. *Minutes of the Twenty-seventh Session of the New England Annual Conference of the African Methodist Episcopal Church.* Boston: J. E. Farwell, 1878.

———. "The New Missionary Law of the African Methodist Episcopal Church." *African Methodist Episcopal Church Review* 13, no. 3 (January 1897).

———. *Preamble and Constitution of the Educational Orphan Institute and Daughters of Salem.* Boston: Geo. C. Rand, 1853.

———. *Proceedings of the Fifteenth Annual Session of the Illinois Annual Conference of the African Methodist Episcopal Church.* Quincy, Ill.: Volk, Jones, and McMein, 1886.

———. *Proceedings of the First Session of the Literary and Historical Society.* Nashville, Tenn.: AME Sunday School Union, 1893.

———. *Proceedings of the Fourteenth Annual Session of the Illinois Annual Conference of the African Methodist Episcopal Church.* Philadelphia: Christian Recorder, 1885.

———. *Proceedings of the Fourth Annual Session of the North Missouri Conference of the African Methodist Episcopal Church.* Philadephia: Christian Recorder, 1885.

———. *Proceedings of the Sixth Session of Kansas Conference African Methodist Episcopal Church.* Kansas City, Mo.: Ramsey, Millett, and Hudson, 1881.

———. *Proceedings of the Twelfth Annual Conference of the African Methodist Episcopal Church.* San Francisco, E. C. Hughes: 1879.

———. *Record of the Bethel African Methodist Episcopal Church.* New York: Carlton and Porter, 1864.

———. *Seventeenth Session and the Sixteenth Quadrennial Session of the General Conference of the African Methodist Episcopal Church.* Xenia, Ohio: Torchlight, 1882.

———. *Thirty-ninth Annual Conference of the African Methodist Episcopal Church of Philadelphia, May 26, 1855.* Philadelphia: n.p., 1855.

———. *The Twenty-first Quadrennial Report of the Home and Foreign Missionary Department of the African Methodist Episcopal Church, 1896–1900.* New York: Bible House, 1900.

GENERAL UNPUBLISHED REFERENCES

Adams, Revels A. *Cyclopedia of African Methodism in Mississippi.* 1902.

Armstrong, William. *Personal Diary.* Manuscript History Society of Pennsylvania, Collection 164, 1872.

Arnett, Benjamin. *The Budget.* 1888.

———. *Budget of 1885–86, Ninth African Methodist Episcopal Church.* 1886.

———. *Centennial, The Budget.* 1889.

———. *Proceedings of the Quarter Centennial Conference of the African Methodist Episcopal Church of South Carolina.* 1890.

Ashmore, Nancy Vance. "The Development of the African Methodist Episcopal Church in South Carolina, 1865–1965." Master's thesis, University of South Carolina, 1969.

Bloom, Jack. *The Negro Church and the Movement for Equality.* Master's thesis, University of California, Berkeley, 1966.

Carter, Ashley B. "A Century of Christian Service." In *Quinn Chapel African Methodist Episcopal Church Centennial Celebration.* Chicago, 1947.

Cheagle, Roslyn V. "The Colored Temperance Movement: 1830–1860." Master's thesis, Department of History, Howard University, Washington, D.C., 1969.

Coppin, Levi J. *A Sketch of the Life of Arthur E. Tate.* 1886.

———. *Reverend, In Memoriam: Catherine S. Campbell-Beckett.* 1888.

Cunningham, Dorothy Holmes. "An Analysis of the A.M.E. Church Review, 1884–1900." Master's thesis, Department of History, Howard University, Washington, D.C., 1950.

Foster, John. *Life and Labors of Mrs. Maggie Newton Van Cott, the First Lady Licensed to Preach in the Methodist Episcopal Church in the United States.* 1872.

Grant, Abraham. *Deaconess Manual of A.M.E. Church.* 1902.

Henry, Thomas W. *Autobiography of Rev. Thomas W. Henry of the African Methodist Episcopal Church.* 1872.

Jarvis, Joseph W. *Golden Jubilee African Methodist Episcopal Church Lansing, Michigan, 1867–1917.* 1917.

Metropolitan African Methodist Episcopal Church. "Notes: History on Various Activities." Manuscript, Metropolitan AME Church Records, folder 11, box 1, Moorland-Spingarn Research Center, Howard University, Washington, D.C., n.d.

Page, Carol A. "Henry McNeal Turner and the 'Ethiopian Movement' in South African 1896–1904." Master's thesis, Roosevelt University, Department of History, 1973.

Polk, Alma A. *Twelve Pioneer Women in the African Methodist Episcopal Church.* 1947.

GENERAL PUBLISHED REFERENCES

Adams, E. A., Sr., ed. *Yearbook and Historical Guide to the African Methodist Episcopal Church.* Rev. ed. Columbia, S.C.: Bureau of Research and History, 1959.

Ahlstrom, Sydney E. *A Religious History of the American People*. New Haven, Conn.:Yale University Press, 1972.

Allen, Richard. *The Life, Experience, and Gospel Labors of the Rt. Rev. Richard Allen*. Philadelphia: F. Ford and M. A. Riply, 1880.

Angell, Stephen Ward. *Bishop Henry McNeal Turner and African-American Religion in the South*. Knoxville: University of Tennessee Press, 1992.

Arnett, B. W. *Proceedings of the Semi-Centenary Celebration of the African Methodist Episcopal Church of Cincinnati*. Cincinnati: H. Watkin, 1874.

Arnett, Benjamin, *The Budget*. Dayton, Ohio: Christian Publishing House, c. 1883.

———. *The Budget of 1904*. Philadelphia: Rev. E. W. Lampton and Rev. J. H. Collett, 1904.

Bacon, Benjamin C. *Statistic of the Colored People of Philadelphia*. Philadelphia: T. Ellwood Chapman, 1856.

———. *Minutes of the First, Second and Third Sessions of the Abbeyville* [sic] *Singing Conventions of the A.M.E. Church*. Abbeville, S.C.: Hugh Wilson, 1889.

Bardolph, Richard. *The Negro Vanguard*. New York: Vintage, 1959.

Bell, Daniel. "The Power Elite: Reconsidered." *The American Journal of Sociology* 64, no. 3 (November 1958): 238–50.

Bergman, Peter M. *The Chronological History of the Negro in America*. New York: New American Library, 1969.

Berlin, Ira, *Slaves without Masters: Free Negro in the Antebellum South*. New York: Vintage, 1974.

Berry, L. L. *A Century of Missions of the African Methodist Episcopal Church, 1840–1940*. New York: Gutenberg, 1942.

Berwanger, Eugene H. *The Frontier against Slavery: Western Anti-Negro Prejudice and the Slavery Extension Controversy*. Chicago: University of Illinois Press, 1967.

Betts, Albert Deems. *History of South Carolina Methodism*. Columbia, S.C.: Advocate, 1952.

Bierstedt, Robert. "An Analysis of Social Power." *The American Sociological Review* 15 (1950): 730–38.

Billingsley, Andrew. *Black Families in White America*. Englewood Cliffs, N.J.: Prentice-Hall, 1968.

Blassingame, John W. *The Slave Community: Plantation Life in the Antebellum South*. New York: Oxford University Press, 1972.

Blau, Peter. "Theories of Organizations." In *International Encyclopedia of the Social Sciences*, edited by David Sills. Vol. 11. New York: Macmillan and Free Press, 1968.

Blauvelt, Martha Tomhave. "Women and Revivalism." In *Women and Religion in America*, edited by Rosemary Reuther and Rosemary Kelly. San Francisco: Harper and Row, 1981.

Blauvelt, Mary Taylor. "The Race Problems as Discussed by Negro Women." *American Journal of Sociology* 6 (1901): 662–72.

Bracey, John H., Jr. "Smith Amanda Berry." In *Notable American Women 1607–1950: A Biographic Dictionary.* Cambridge, Mass.: Harvard University Press, 1971.

Brackett, Jeffrey. *The Negro in Maryland.* New York: Negro Universities Press, 1889.

Bragg, George F., Jr. *Men of Maryland.* Baltimore: Church Advocate, 1925.

Broderick, Francis C., and August Meier, eds. *Negro Protest Thought in the Twentieth Century.* New York: Bobbs-Merrill, 1965.

Brown, Elsa Barkley. "Womanist Consciousness: Maggie Lena Walker and the Independent Order of Saint Luke." *Signs: Journal of Women in Culture and Society* 14, no. 3 (Spring 1989): 610–33.

Brown, Hallie Q. *Homespun Heroines and Other Women of Distinction.* Xenia, Ohio: Aldine, 1926.

Butt, Israel L., D.D. Rev., *History of African Methodism in Virginia or Four Decades in the Old Dominion.* Hampton, Va.: Hampton Institute Press, 1908.

Campbell, Jabez P. "The Ordination of Women: What's the Authority for It?" *AME Church Review* 11, no. 4 (1886): 351–61.

Campbell, Jabez P., ed. *Doctrines and Discipline of the African Methodist Episcopal Church.* Philadelphia: Wm. S. Young, 1856.

Campbell, James T. *Songs of Zion: The African Methodist Episcopal Church in the United States and South Africa.* Chapel Hill: University of North Carolina Press, 1998.

Carroll, Berenice A. "Peace Research: The Cult of Power." *Journal of Conflict Resolution* 16 (1972): 585–616.

——. *Liberating Women's History.* Chicago: University of Illinois Press, 1976.

Cartwright, Dorwin. *Studies in Social Power.* Ann Arbor: University of Michigan, 1959.

Cary, Mary Ann Shadd. "Mary Ann Shadd-Cary 1823–1893, the Foremost Colored Canadian Pioneer in 1859." Manuscript, Mary Ann Shadd-Cary Papers, folder 4, box 1, Moorland-Spingarn Research Center, Howard University, Washington, D.C., n.d.

——. "Trifles." *Anglo-African Magazine* 1 (1859): 55–56.

——. "Statement of Purpose: Colored Women's Progressive Franchise Association." Manuscript, Mary Ann Shadd-Cary Papers, folder 5, box 1, Moorland-Spingarn Research Center, Howard University, Washington, D.C., c. 1880.

——. "Speech of Judiciary Committee re: The Rights of Women to Vote." Manuscript, Mary Ann Shadd-Cary Papers, folder 2, box 1, Moorland-Spingarn Research Center, Howard University, Washington, D.C., c. 1890.

Clark, Elmer T. *The Negro and His Religion*. Nashville, Tenn.: Cokes-
berry, 1924.

Collins, Patricia Hill. "The Social Construction of Black Feminist
Thought." *Signs: Journal of Women in Culture and Society* 14, no. 14
(Summer 1989): 745–73.

———. *Black Feminist Thought: Knowledge, Consciousness, Politics of
Empowerment*. Boston: Unwin Hyman, 1990.

Connolly, Harold X. *Blacks in Brooklyn from 1900–1960* . Ph.D. dissertation, New York University, 1972.

Cook, John F. "Extract of Proceedings Annual Conference of the
African Methodist Episcopal Church for the Baltimore District,
Washington City, April 28, 1840." Manuscript, Cook Family Papers,
box 1, Moorland-Spingarn Research Center, Howard University,
Washington, D.C., 1840.

———. "Outstanding Members of the First Church, September 1, 1840,"
Manuscript, Cook Family Papers, box 1, Moorland-Spingarn Research Center, Howard University, Washington, D.C.

Cook, Karen S. "Exchange and Power in Networks of Interorganiza-
tional Relations." *The Sociological Quarterly,* no. 18 (1977): 62–82.

Cooper, Anna J. "The Higher Education of Women." *The Southland* 2
(1891): 186–202.

———. *A Voice from the South by A Black Woman of the South*. Xenia,
Ohio: Aldine, 1892.

———. "In Behalf of the Women of St. Luke's Church." In *The Shades
and the Lights of a Fifty Years' Ministry, 1844–1894*. Washington,
D.C.: R. L. Pendleton, 1894.

Coppin, Fanny Jackson. *Reminiscences of School Life and Hints on
Teaching*. Philadelphia: AME Book Concern, 1913.

Cornish, John. *Opinion of the Supreme Court of Pennsylvania in the
Case of the Commonwealth ex. Relatione Miller et al. vs. Rev. John
Cornish*. Philadelphia: J. D. Oliver and Rev. J. P. B. Eddey, 1858.

Crogman, W. H., and J. W. Gibson. *Progress of a Race*. Naperville, Ill.:
J.C. Nichols, 1902.

Cromwell, John W. "First Negro Churches in the District of Columbia."
Journal of Negro History 7, no. 1 (January 1922).

Crozier, Michel. "The Problem of Power," *Social Research* 40, no. 2
(Summer 1973).

Crummell, Alex. *African and American: Addresses and Discourses*.
Springfield, Mass.: Willey, 1891.

Culp, Daniel W. *Twentieth Century Negro Literature*. New York: Arno,
1969.

Culver, Dwight W. *Negro Segregation on the Methodist Church*. New
Haven, Conn.: Yale University Press, 1953.

Dahl, Robert A. "Power." In *International Encyclopedia of the Social Sciences,* edited by David Sill. New York: Macmillan and Free Press, 1968.

Daniel, Sadie Iola. *Women Builders.* Washington, D.C.: Associated, 1931.

Dannett, Sylvia G. L. *Profiles of Negro Womanhood.* Vol. 1. Chicago: Educational Heritage, 1964.

Davis, Elizabeth Lindsay. *Lifting as They Climb.* N.p.: National Association of Colored Women, 1933.

Davis, W. R. *Annual Missionary Album of the African Methodist Episcopal Church.* Vol 1. New York: Hunt and Eaton, 1895.

Delany, Martin R. *Eulogy on the Life and Character of the Rev. Fayette Davis.* Pittsburgh: Berry Franklin Peterson, 1847.

Dill, Bonnie. "The Dialectics of Black Womanhood." *Signs: Journal of Women in Culture and Society* (1980): 343–550.

Dodson, Jualynne E. "Women's Collective Power in the AME Church." Ph.D. dissertation, University of California, Berkeley, 1984.

——. "A Look at the Past." *The AME Church Review* (January–March 1989): 9–18.

Domhoff, William, and Hoyt B. Ballard. *C. Wright Mills and the Power Elite.* Boston: Beacon, 1968.

Doyle, Bertram Wilbur. *The Etiquette of Race Relations in the South: A Study of Social Control.* Chicago: University of Chicago Press, 1937.

Drake, St. Clair. *Churches and Voluntary Associations in the Chicago Community.* Chicago: Works Progress Administration District 8, 1940.

Drake, St. Clair, and Horace R. Cayton. *Black Metropolis: A Study of Negro Life in a Northern City.* Vol. 2. New York: Harper and Row, 1945.

Duberman, Lucile. *Gender and Sex in Society.* New York: Praeger, 1975.

DuBois, W. E. B. *The Philadelphia Negro: A Social Study.* New York: Schocken, 1899.

——. *The Negro Church.* Atlanta: Atlanta University Press, 1903.

——. *Efforts for Social Betterment among Negro Americans.* Atlanta: Atlanta University Press, 1909.

——. *Black Reconstruction in America.* New York: Harcourt, Brace, 1935.

Duncan, Sara J. "Woman a Factor in the Development of Christian Missions." In *Journal of the 21st Quadrennial Session of the General Confrence of the African M.E. Church.* Philadelphia: AME Book Concern, 1900.

——. "Vital Questions: Our Missionary Department." *Christian Recorder,* December 3, 1903.

——. *Progressive Missions in the South: An Address with Illustrations and Sketches of Missionary Workers and Ministers and Bishops Wives.* Atlanta: Franklin, 1906.

Dunlap, Mollie E., and Anne O'H. Williamson, eds. *Institutions of Higher Learning among Negroes in the United States of America: A Compendium.* Yellow Springs, Ohio: Wilberforce University, 1947.

Elaw, Zilpha. *Memoirs of the Life, Religious Experience, Ministerial Travels and Labours of Mrs. Zilpha Elaw: An American Female of Colour.* London: n.p., 1846.

Emerson, Richard M. "Exchange Theory, Part II: Exchange Relations, Exchange Networks and Groups as Exchange Systems." In *Sociological Theories in Progress,* edited by Joseph Berger, Morris Zelditch, and Bo Anderson. Vol. 2. Boston: Houghton Mifflin, 1972.

Fauset, Arthur H. *Black Gods of the Metropolis.* Philadelphia: University of Pennsylvania Press, 1944.

Fickling, Susan M. *Slave Conversion in South Carolina 1830–1860.* Columbia: University of South Carolina Press, 1924.

Fraizer, E. Franklin. *The Negro in the United States.* 2d ed. New York: Macmillan, 1967.

———. *The Negro Church in America.* New York: Schocken, 1963.

Franklin, John Hope. *From Slavery to Freedom: A History of Negro Americans.* New York: Vintage, 1969.

French, John R. P., Jr., and Bertram Raven. "The Bases of Social Power." In *Studies in Social Power,* edited by Dorwin Cartwright. Ann Arbor: University of Michigan, Institute for Social Research, 1959.

Gaines, Wesley John. *African Methodism in the South.* Atlanta: Franklin, 1890.

Gerber, David A. *Black Ohio and the Color Line, 1816–1915.* University of Illinois Press: Chicago.

Gibson, A. B. B. *The African Methodist Shield Improved.* Macon, Ga.: n.p., 1919.

Glock, Charles, Benjamin Ringer, and Earl Babbie. *To Comfort and to Challenge.* Berkeley: University of California Press, 1976.

Goldhamer, Herbert, and Edward Shils. "Types of Power and Status." *The American Journal of Sociology* 45 (1939): 171–82.

Gordon, Ann D., Mari Jo Buhle, and Nancy Schromdize. "The Problem of Women's History." In *Liberating Women's History,* edited by Berenice Carroll. Urbana: University of Illinois Press, 1976.

Green, A. R. *The Life of Rev. Dandridge F. Davis of the African Methodist Episcopal Church. Also A Brief Sketch of the Life of Rev. David Conyou.* Pittsburgh: n.p., 1853.

Griffin, Eunice. *Rise of American Missions: The African Methodist Episcopal Church.* New York: Coker, 1960.

Gullins, William R. *The Heroes of the Virginia Annual Conference of the African Methodist Episcopal Church.* Smithfield, Va.: n.p., 1899.

Gustafason, Berndt, "Types of Religious Institutionalization." In *Institutionalism and Church Unity*, edited by Nils Ehrenstrom and Walter Muelder. New York: Associated Press, 1963.

Haley, James T. *Afro-American Encyclopaedia*. Nashville, Tenn.: Haley and Florida, 1896.

Handy, James A. *Scraps of African Methodist Episcopal History*. Philadelphia: AME Book Concern, n.d.

Hanson, J. W., ed. *World's Congress of Religions*. Proceedings of a Conference Held in the Art Institute, Chicago, August 25–October 15, 1893, under the auspices of the World's Columbian Exposition International. Chicago: n.p., 1894.

Harrison, Paul M. *Authority and Power in the Free Church Tradition*. Princeton, N.J.: Princeton University Press, 1959.

———. "Weber's Categories of Authority and Voluntary Associations." *American Sociological Review* 25 (1960): 232–37.

Harrison, William Pope. *The Gospel among the Slaves. A Short Account of Missionary Operations among the African Slaves of the Southern States*. Nashville, Tenn.: Publishing House of the Methodist Episcopal Church South, 1893.

Hartzell, Joseph C. "Methodism and the Negro in the United States." *Journal of Negro History* 8, no. 3 (July 1923).

Heard, William H. *From Slavery to the Bishopric in the Church*. New York: Acme and New York Times, 1924. Reprint, 1969.

Herberg, Will. *Protestant-Catholic-IEW*. Garden City, N.Y.: Anchor and Doubleday, 1955.

Hicks, Henry Beecher, Jr. *Images of the Black Preacher: The Man Nobody Knows*. Valley Forge, Pa.: Judson, 1977.

Higginbotham, Evelyn Brooks. *Righteous Discontent: The Women's Movement in the Black Baptist Church, 1880–1920*. Cambridge, Mass.: Harvard University Press, 1983.

Higginbotham, Elizabeth. "Two Representative Issues in Contemporary Sociological Work on Black Women." In *But Some of Us Were Brave*, edited by Gloria T. Hull, Patricia Bell Scott, and Barbara Smith. Old Westbury, N.Y.: Feminist, 1982.

Hiller, Dana V., and Robin Ann Sheets. *Women and Men: The Consequences of Power*. Cincinnati: University of Cincinnati, 1977.

Hine, Darlene Clark, ed., Elsa Barkley Brown and Rosalyn Terborg-Penn, assoc. eds. *Black Women in America: An Historical Encyclopedia*. Brooklyn, N.Y.: Carlson, 1993.

Hobson, Elizabeth, and Charlotte Everett Hopkins. *A Report Concerning the Colored Women of the South*. Trustees of the John F. Slater Fund, Occasional Paper no. 9. Baltimore: n.p., 1896.

Hood, J. W. *One Hundred Years of the African Methodist Episcopal Zion Church.* New York: AME Book Concern, 1895.

Illinois Writers Project. "Churches: Organizations and Conventions." Vivian G. Harsh Collection of the Carter G. Woodson Branch, box 29, Chicago Public Library, Chicago, 1939.

——. "Churches: Organizations and Conventions." Vivian G. Harsh Collection of the Carter G. Woodson Branch, box 33, Chicago Public Library, Chicago, 1940.

——. "Churches: Organizations and Conventions." Vivian G. Harsh of the Carter G. Woodson Branch, box 28, Chicago Public Library, Chicago, 1941.

Jackson, Rebecca. *Gifts of Power: The Writings of Rebecca Jackson, Black Visionary, Shaker Eldress.* Edited by Jean McMahon Humez. Amherst: University of Massachusetts Press, 1981.

Jackson, Thomas Henry. *Sketch of the Life and Character of Rev. Simon Miler, Presiding Elder of the Columbia District, South Carolina Annual Conference, African Methodist Episcopal Church.* Columbia, S.C.: Union-Herald, 1875.

Jacobs, Sylvia M., and Paul R. Dekar, eds. *Black Americans and the Missionary Movement in Africa.* Westport, Conn.: Greenwood, 1982.

Jacquet, Constant, Jr., ed. *Yearbook of American and Canadian Churches.* Nashville, Tenn.: Abingdon, 1982.

Janowitz, Morris. "Hierarchy and Authority in the Military Establishment." In *Complex Organizations,* ed. Amitai Etzioni. New York: Holt, Rinehart, and Winston, 1962.

Jenifer, John T. *Centennial Retrospect History of the African Methodist Episcopal Church.* Nashville, Tenn.: Sunday School Union, c. 1912.

Johnson, Clifton H., ed. *God Struck Me Dead.* Philadelphia: Pilgrim, 1969.

——. "Mary Ann Shadd: Crusader for the Freedom of Man." *Crisis* 78, no. 3 (1971): 90.

Johnston, Ronald L. "Negro Preachers Take Sides." *Review of Religious Research* 2 (Fall 1969): 81–89.

Kanter, Rosabeth Moss. *Men and Women of the Corporation.* New York: Basic, 1977.

Kanter, Rosabeth M., and Barry A. Stein. *Life in Organizations.* New York: Basic, 1979.

Kuhn, Alfred. Review of "Exchange and Power in Social Life," by Peter Blau. *Science* 147, no. 137 (1965).

——. "On Making Power a Tight Analytic Tool." Paper presented at meeting of *American Sociological Association,* Boston, 1979.

Lampton, Edward W. *Digest of Ruling and Decisions of the Bishops of the African Methodist Episcopal Church from 1847–1907.* Washington, D.C.: Record, 1907.

Lee, Benjamin F. "The Quadrennial Report of the President of Wilberforce University." In *Seventeenth Session and the Sixteenth Quadrennial Session of the General Conference of the African Methodist Episcopal Church*, ed. B. Arnett. Xenia, Ohio: Torchlight, 1880.

Lee, Jarena Mrs. *The Religious Experience and Journal of Mrs. Jarena Lee: Giving an Account of Her Call to Preach the Gospel.* Philadelphia: n.p., 1849.

Lewis, Rev. G. *Impression of America and the American Churches: From Journal of the Rev. G. Lewis.* New York: Negro Universities Press, 1848. Reprint, 1968.

Lincoln, C. Eric, and Lawrence H. Mamiya. *The Black Church in the African American Experience.* Durham, N.C.: Duke University Press, 1990.

Litwak, Leon. *North of Slavery: The Negro in the Free States, 1790–1860.* Chicago: University of Chicago Press, 1961.

Loewenberg, Bert James, and Ruth Bogin. *Black Women in Nineteenth-Century American Life.* University Park: Pennsylvania State University Press, 1976.

Lofton, John. *Insurrection in South Carolina: The Turbulent World of Denmark Vessey.* Yellow Spring, Ohio: Antioch, 1964.

Long, Charles Sumner. *History of the African Methodist Episcopal Church in Florida.* Philadelphia: AME Book Concern, 1939.

Lyman, Stanford M. *The Black American in Sociological Thought.* New York: Capricorn, 1973.

McManus, Edgar J. *History of Negro Slavery in New York.* Syracuse, N.Y.: Syracuse University Press, 1966.

McTyeire, Holland N. *A History of Methodism: Comprising a View of the Rise of This Revival of Spiritual Religion in the First Half of the Eighteenth Century and of the Principal Agents by Whom It Was Promoted in Europe and America.* Nashville, Tenn.: Southern Methodist, 1884.

Majors, Monroe A. *Noted Negro Women: Their Triumphs and Activities.* Freeport, N.Y.: Books for Libraries, 1893. Reprint, 1971.

Makler, Harry M. "Centralization/Decentralization in Formal Organizations: A Case Study of America. Protestant Denominations." *Review of Religious Research* 5 (1963): 5–11.

Mathews, Marcia M. *Richard Allen.* Baltimore: Helicon, 1963.

Mays, Benjamin E. *The Negro's God: As Reflected in His Literature.* New York: Atheneum, 1938.

Mays, Benjamin, and Joseph Nicholeson. *The Negro's Church.* New York: Arno, 1933. Reprinted 1969.

Methodist Episcopal Church. *The Doctrines and Discipline of the Methodist Episcopal Church.* New York: J. Collard, 1832.

———. *Minutes of the Annual Conferences of the Methodist Episcopal Church South for the Year 1862.* Nashville, Tenn.: Southern Methodist, 1870.

———. *Minutes of the Annual Conferences of the Methodist Episcopal Church South for the Year 1863.* Nashville, Tenn.: Southern Methodist, 1870.

———. *Minutes of the Annual Conferences of the Methodist Episcopal Church South for the Year 1864.* Nashville, Tenn.: Southern Methodist, 1870.

———. *Minutes of the Annual Conferences of the Methodist Episcopal Church South for the Year 1865.* Nashville, Tenn.: Southern Methodist, 1870.

———. *Minutes of the Annual Conferences of the Methodist Episcopal Church South for the Year 1866.* Nashville, Tenn.: Southern Methodist, 1870.

———. *Minutes of the South Carolina Conference of the Methodist Episcopal Church South for 1864. 1865, 1866.* Charleston, S.C.: Weekly Record, 1867.

Meyer, Annie Nathan, *Woman's Work in America.* New York: Arno, 1891. Reprint, 1972.

Meyer, John W., and Brian Rowan. "Institutionalized Organizations: Formal Structure as Myth and Ceremony." *American Journal of Sociology* 83 (September 1977): 340–63.

Miles, William Porcher. *Women "Nobly Planned": How to Educate Our Girls.* Pamphlet address, c. 1885.

Mixon, Rev. Winfield Henri. *History of the African Methodist Episcopal Church in Alabama.* Nashville, Tenn.: AME Church Sunday School Union, 1902.

Moore, R. *History of Bethel African Methodist Episcopal Church, Chicago, U.S.A.* Chicago: Fraternal, n.d.

Morant, John J. *Mississippi Minister.* New York: Vantage, 1958.

Morgan, Joseph. *Morgan's History of the New Jersey Conference of the African Methodist Episcopal Church from 1872–1887.* Camden, N.J.: S. Chew, 1887.

Mossell, Gertrude N. F. *The Work of the Afro-American Woman.* Philadelphia: Geo. S. Ferguson, 1908.

Mott, A. *Biographical Sketches and Interesting Anecdotes of Persons of Color: To Which Is Added a Selection of Pieces in Poetry.* 2d ed. New York: Mahlon Day, 1837.

Murray, Florence, ed. *The Negro Handbook: A Manual of Current Facts, Statistics and General Information Concerning Negroes in the United States.* New York: Current Reference, 1944.

National Woman Suffrage Association. *Report of the International Council of Women.* Washington, D.C.: Rufus H. Darby, 1888.

Nelsen, Hart M., Anne K. Nelsen, and Raytha L. Yokley, eds. *The Black Church in America.* New York: Basic, 1971.

Newton, Alexander Herritage. *Out of the Briars: An Autobiography and Sketch of the Twenty-ninth Regiment Connecticut Volunteers.* Philadelphia: AME Book Concern, 1910.

Norwood, Frederick A. *The Story of American Methodism: A History of the United Methodists and Their Relations.* Nashville, Tenn.: Abingdon, 1974.

O'Reilly, Henry. *Settlement in the West: Sketches of Rochester with Incidental Notices of Western New York.* Rochester, N.Y.: William Alling, 1838.

Ovington, Mary White. *Half a Man: The Status of the Negro in New York.* New York: Longmans, Green, 1911.

Payne, Daniel A. *The Semi-Centenary and the Retrospection of the African Methodist Episcopal Church in the United States.* Baltimore: Sherwood, 1866.

———. *History of the African Methodist Episcopal Church.* Nashville, Tenn.: African Methodist Sunday School Union, 1891.

———. *Recollections of Seventy Years.* New York: Arno, 1968.

Payne, Ethel. "City's 2 Oldest Churches Quinn 106—Olivet 92." *Chicago Defender,* February 14, 1953.

Pipes, William H. *Say Amen Brother.* New York: William Frederick, 1951.

Pitts, Walter E. *Old Ship of Zion: The Afro-Baptist Ritual in the African Diaspora.* New York: Oxford, 1993.

Ponton, M. M. *Life and Times of Henry M. Turner.* Atlanta: A. B. Caldwell, 1917.

Powers, Bernard E. Jr. *Black Charlestonians: A Social History 1822–1885.* Fayetteville: University of Arkansas Press, 1994.

Raboteau, Albert J. *Slave Religion: The "Invisible Institution" in the Antebellum South.* New York: Oxford University Press, 1978.

Ransom, Reverdy C. *The Pilgrimage of Harriet Ransom's Son.* Nashville, Tenn.: Sunday School Union, c. 1950.

———. "Confessions of a Bishop." *Ebony* (March 1950): 72–80.

———. *Preface to History of African Methodist Episcopal Church.* Nashville, Tenn.: AME Sunday School Union, 1950.

Raven, Charles E. *Women and the Ministry.* Garden City, N.Y.: Doubleday and Doran, 1929.

Richardson, Harry V. *Dark Salvation: The Story of Methodism as It Developed among Blacks in America.* New York: Anchor, 1976.

Richey, Russell, ed. *Denominationalism.* Nashville, Tenn.: Abingdon, 1977.

Ringer, Bejamin B. *"We the People" and Others: Duality and America's Treatment of Its Racial Minority.* London: Tavistock, 1983.

Rodgers-Rose, La Frances, ed. *The Black Woman.* Beverly Hills, Calif.: Sage, 1980.

Rose, Arnold. *The Power Structure.* New York: Oxford University Press, 1967.

Schermerhorn, Richard A. *Society and Power.* New York: Random House, 1961.

Scruggs, Lawson Anderson. *Women of Distinction.* Raleigh, N.C.: L. A. Scruggs, 1893.

Sernett, Milton C. *Black Religion and American Evangelicalism.* Metuchen, N.J.: Scarecrow, 1975.

Shipp, Albert M. *History of Methodism in South Carolina.* Nashville, Tenn.: Southern Methodist House, 1883.

Shorter, Aylward W. F., ed. *African Christian Spirituality.* New York: Orbis, 1978.

Sikes, Walter W. "The Principle of Authority and the Heritage of a Free Church." *Encounter* 33, no. 1 (Winter 1972): 112–27.

Sills, David, ed. *International Encyclopedia of the Social Sciences.* New York: Macmillan and Free Press, 1968.

Simmel, Georg, "Domination, a Form of Interaction." *The Sociology of Georg Simmel,* edited and translated by Kurt H. Wolff. Glencoe, Ill.: Free Press, 1950.

Singleton, George A. *The Romance of African Methodism: A Study of the African Methodist Episcopal Church.* New York: Exposition, 1952.

———. *Sarah Allen: A Portrait of the Heroine Mother of African Methodism.* Pamphlet. N.p., 1960.

———. *Autobiography of George A. Singleton.* Boston: Forum, 1964.

Smith, Amanda Berry. *Amanda Smith: The Colored Evangelist.* Chicago: Christian Witness, 1921.

Smith, Charles S. *Dedicatory Services at the Publishing House of the African Methodist Episcopal Church Sunday School Union held January 20–21, 1889.* Nashville, Tenn.: AME Sunday School Union, 1894.

———. *A History of the African Methodist Episcopal Church.* Philadelphia: Book Concern of the AME Church, 1922.

Smith, David. *Biography of Rev. David Smith of the African Methodist Episcopal Church.* Xenia, Ohio: Xenia Gazette, 1881.

Smith, H. Shelton. *In His Image, But . . . : Racism in Southern Religion, 1780–1910.* Durham, N.C.: Duke University Press, 1972.

South Carolina African Methodist Episcopal Church. *Minutes of the South Carolina Annual Conference of the African Methodist Episco-*

pal Church 1865, 1866, 1867. Charleston, S.C.: Charleston Messenger. Reprint, J. E. Beard, 1914.

Steady, Filomina. "African and African American Feminism." In *Women in Africa and the African Diaspora*, edited by Rosalyn Terborg-Penn et al., 3–24. Washington, D.C.: Howard University Press, 1987.

Stevens, Abel. *Women of Methodism*. New York: Carlton and Porter, 1866.

Steward, Theophilus Gould *Fifty Years in the Gospel Ministry*. Philadelphia: AME Book Concern, c. 1915.

———. *Memoirs of Mrs. Rebecca Steward*. Philadelphia: Publication Department, AME Church, 1877.

Steward, William, and Theophilus Gould Steward. *Gouldtown, a Very Remarkable Settlement of Ancient Date*. Philadelphia: Lippincott, 1913.

Takayama, J. Peter, and Lynn Weber Cannon. "Formal Polity and Power Distribution in American Protestant Denominations." *The Sociological Quarterly* (Summer 1979): 331–32.

Taylor, A. A. "The Negro in South Carolina during the Reconstruction." *Journal of Negro History* 9, no. 3 (July 1924): 245–58.

Taylor, Marshall W. *Life, Travels, Labors and Helpers of Mrs. Amanda Smith, the Famous Negro Missionary Evangelist*. Cincinnati: Cranston and Stowe, 1887.

Taylor, Susie King. *Reminiscences of My Life in Camp with the 33d United States Colored Troops Late 1st S.C. Volunteers*. Boston: n.p., 1902.

Taylor, William. *Story of My Life*. New York: Hunt and Eaton, 1896.

Terborg-Penn, Rosalyn, Sharon Harley, and Andrea Benton Rushing. *Women in Africa and the African Diaspora*. Washington, D.C.: Howard University Press, 1987.

Thompson, James D. "Authority and Power in 'Identical' Organizations." *American Journal of Sociology* 62, no. 3 (November 1956): 290–301.

Thompson, Joseph S. *Bethel Gleanings*. Philadelphia: Robert J. Holland, 1881.

Thornton, John A. "The History of St. James African Methodist Episcopal Church." In *A Century of African Methodism in the Deep South*. New Orleans: St. James African Methodist Episcopal Church, c. 1946.

Townsend, Vince M. *Fifty-four Years of African Methodism*. New York: Exposition Press, 1953.

Tucker, David M. *Black Pastors and Leaders: Memphis, 1819–1972*. Memphis, Tenn.: Memphis State University Press, 1975.

Turner, Edward Raymond. *The Negro in Pennsylvania: Slavery-Servitude-Freedom, 1639–1861*. American Historical Association: Washington, D.C., 1911.

Turner, Henry McNeal. *The Genius and Theory of Methodist Polity or the Machinery of Methodism*. Philadelphia: Publication Department of the AME Church, 1885.

———. "Letter of Bishop Henry M. Turner Written during His Visit to Africa." *African Methodist Episcopal Church Review* 8, no. 4 (April 1891).

Urban Media Research Associates. "Dollars and Sense Religious Survey Results." *Dollars and Sense* 7, no. 2 (1981): 60–62.

U.S. Census. *Abstract of the Twelfth Census of the United States, 1900*. Washington, D.C.: Government Printing Office, 1902.

———. *Census for 1820*. Washington, D.C.: n.p., 1821.

———. *A Compendium of the Ninth Census June 1, 1870*. Washington, D.C.: Government Printing Office, 1872.

———. *A Compendium of the Tenth Census June 1, 1880*. Washington, D.C.: Government Printing Office, 1883.

———. *Population of the United States in 1860: Compiled from the Original Return of the Eighth Census*. Washington, D.C.: Government Printing Office, 1864.

———. *Religious Bodies 1916: Part I, Summary and General Tables*. Washington, D.C.: Government Printing Office, 1916.

———. *Religious Bodies 1916: Part II, Separate Denominations History, Descriptions and Statistics*. Washington, D.C.: Government Printing Office, 1916.

U.S. Treasury Department. *Aggregate Amount of Persons within the United States in the Year 1810*. Washington, D.C.: Treasury Department, 1811.

Voegeli, V. Jacques. *Free but Not Equal: The Mid-West and the Negro during the Civil War*. Chicago: University of Chicago, 1967.

Voice of Missions 36, no. 26 (January 1930).

Voice of Missions 52, no. 2 (February 1941).

Von Wiese, [complete name unknown] et al. "Institutionalization." *Readings in Sociology*, edited by Alfred M. Lee. New York: Barnes and Noble, 1951.

Walls, William J. *The African Methodist Episcopal Zion Church: Reality of the Black Church*. Charlotte, N.C.: African Methodist Zion, 1974.

Washington, Mary Helen. *Invented Lives: Narratives of Black Women 1860–1960*. Garden City, N.Y.: Anchor, 1987.

Wayman, Alexander Walker. *My Recollections of African Methodist Episcopal Minutes, or Forty Years' Experience in the African Methodist Episcopal Church*. Philadelphia: AME Book Rooms, 1882.

———. *Cyclopaedia of African Methodism*. Baltimore: Methodist Episcopal Book Depository, 1882.

——. *Manual or Guide Book for the Administration of the Discipline.* Philadelphia: AME Book Rooms, 1886.

——. *The Life of Rev. James Alexander Shorter: One of the Bishops of the African Methodist Episcopal Church.* Baltimore: J. Lanahan, 1890.

Weber, Max. *The Protestant Ethic and the Spirit of Capitalism.* New York: Scribner, 1958.

——. *The Theory of Social and Economic Organization.* Translated by A. M. Henderson and Talcott Parsons. Glencoe, Ill.: Free Press, 1947 [1922].

Weisenfeld, Judith. "The Harlem YWCA and the Secular City, 1904–1945." *Journal of Women's History* 6, no. 3: 2–78.

Wesley, Charles. *Richard Allen, Apostle of Freedom.* Washington, D.C.: Associated, 1935.

Wharton, Vernon L. *The Negro in Mississippi, 1865–1890.* New York: Harper Torchbooks, 1947.

Wheeler, Edward L. *Uplifting the Race: The Black Minister in the New South, 1865–1902.* Lanham, Md.: University Press of America, 1986.

Whiteman, Maxwell, ed. *Articles of Association of the African Methodist Episcopal Church or The City of Philadelphia in the Commonwealth of Pennsylvania.* Philadelphia: Rhestoric, 1969.

Woodson, Carter G. *The History of the Negro Church.* Washington, D.C.: Associated, 1921.

Work, Monroe N. *Negro Year Book and Annual Encyclopedia of the Negro.* Tuskegee, Ala.: Tuskegee Normal and Industrial Institute, 1912.

Wright, Richard R., Jr. *The Bishops of the African Methodist Episcopal Church.* Nashville, Tenn.: AME Sunday School Union, 1963.

——. *Centennial Encyclopaedia of the African Methodist Episcopal Church.* Philadelphia: AME Book Concern, 1916.

——. *The Encyclopaedia of the American Methodist Episcopal Church.* Philadelphia: AME Book Concern, 1947.

——. *The Negro in Pennsylvania: A Study in Economic History.* Philadelphia: AME Book Concern, n.d.

Yinger, J. Milton. *Religion in the Struggle for Power.* New York: Russell and Russell, 1961.

Young, Frank A. "Amanda Smith's Life Work Ends: Succumbs to Paralysis." *Chicago Defender* 10, no. 10 (March 6, 1915).

Index

About the Author

Jualynne E. Dodson is associate professor of African American and religious studies at the University of Colorado. She is also the founder and director of the African Atlantic Research Team in the Department of Ethnic Studies at the University. She publishes regularly on issues of African Americans, women, and African-based religious traditions.